Path to Prosperity

Path to Prosperity

Discovering Biblical Secrets to Build Wealth and Prosperity

Jeanel Champion

The Teaching Ministry of Jeanel D. Champion
www.JeanelChampion.com

Copyright © Jeanel Champion 2021.
All rights reserved.

This book or any portion of it may not be reproduced or used in any manner whatsoever without the express written permission of the author except for the use of brief quotations in a book review or in teaching, where the author is given full credit.

Scripture quotations marked (NKJV) are taken from The Holy Bible, The New King James Version. Copyright © 1982 by Thomas Nelson, Inc. All rights reserved.

Scripture quotations marked (KJV) are taken from The Holy Bible, King James Version.

Scripture quotations marked (NIV) are taken from The Holy Bible, New International Version®. NIV®. Copyright © 1973, 1978, 1984, 2011 by Biblica.

Scripture quotations marked (NLT) are taken from The Holy Bible, New Living Translation. Copyright© 1996, 2004, 2015 by Tyndale House Foundation. Used by permission of Tyndale House Publishers Inc., Carol Stream, Illinois 60188. All rights reserved.

Scripture quotations marked (TPT) are from The Passion Translation®. Copyright © 2017, 2018 by Passion & Fire Ministries, Inc. Used by permission. All rights reserved. ThePassionTranslation.com.

Scripture quotations marked (AMP) are taken from the Amplified Bible, Copyright © 1954, 1958, 1962, 1964, 1965, 1987 by The Lockman Foundation. Used by permission.

Scripture quotations marked (BSB) are taken from The Holy Bible, Berean Study Bible, BSB. Copyright ©2016, 2018 by Bible Hub. Used by Permission. All Rights Reserved Worldwide.

Table of Contents

Acknowledgments 1

The Foundation 3

1. Mind Set 7
2. A Love Affair 27
3. Know Your God 41
4. Breaking the Curse of Poverty 51
5. Restoration 71
6. A Healthy Relationship with Money 105
7. Wealth's Greatest Secret 147
8. The Destruction of Fear 169
9. The Faith and Mouth Connection 179
10. Go Forward 189

A letter to myself 197

ACKNOWLEDGEMENTS

To the Spirit of God, my Best Friend and longest partner, thank You for inspiring this book and giving me the words to say and the courage to step out.

To my editors, my husband Terrell Champion, and my sister in love, Kishma J. Andrew, thank you for your time and efforts in editing this book.

An extra special thank you to my husband again, who has always supported me and promoted my career, advancement, and ministry.

To my beloved children, Isaiah and Aliyah, who were patient to share my time to devote to this book. You are my heart and the joy of my life.

To my parents for raising me to know the Lord and to pursue Him with passion. You taught me to pray, fast, study the Word, and live boldly for Christ, unapologetic.

To all my siblings and their families. Thank you for being there, for praying for me, and for covering me.

ACKNOWLEDGEMENTS

THE FOUNDATION

My greatest desire is for you to know God and to love and serve Him with all your heart. It is very important to understand the truth about God's plan concerning every area of your life such as ministry, career, family, community, and even your finances. Yes, God has a plan for your finances, and He wants to reveal it to you. I am making this clear from the get-go – I am not all about money nor do I want you to be. Over the years, speaking on the topic of prosperity, specifically money, has gotten a bad reputation in the Church. While we should not put money above God, we need to understand this – God wants us to prosper and to excel in all that we do, and our finances are not excluded from this.

Wealth and riches are part of God's plan for His Church, and if you do not agree with me, keep reading and you will have that same revelation.

First, I want you to know this:

The purpose of this book is to set you up to prosper the way God intended!

There is a path that God has lined up for you to follow and you must walk in that path to experience the abundant life He has for you.

Second, before we dive in, I want you to understand the definition of prosperity. According to Merriam Webster's dictionary, prosperity is "the condition of being successful or thriving." To prosper means to be successful in an activity and to flourish. It is to arrive at the level where you are growing abundantly and excelling in what God has designated for you to do.

God does not only want you to prosper financially; God wants you to prosper spiritually, martially, mentally, and physically. He wants you to prosper in your ministry, in your relationships, and your heart and mind; He wants you to be full of peace and joy. If you are married or desire marriage in the future, God wants you to prosper as a wife or husband. If you are or will be a parent, God wants you to prosper in your parenting and build a strong family. He wants you to thrive in your career and business, in your education and learning, and in everything that matters to you – from the smallest to the biggest area in your life. While the principles in this book can lead to prosperity in all areas of your life, the primary focus of this book is financial prosperity. Why?

God instructed me to write this book to prepare you for the wealth He wants to release unto you. God has told me and showed me many times that He has great wealth stored up for His people and He is ready to release it, but many are not prepared to receive this great wealth.

As you walk through this book, you will learn **Wealth's Greatest Secret** and have a plan to build a prosperous future for you, your children, and future generations. I believe that the Holy Spirit is with you and that He will speak to you through this book. You will learn to shed the wrong mindset and take on the correct view of wealth and your finances. Ready? Let us get started!

CHAPTER 1

Mind Set

"For as a man thinks in his heart, so is he."
Proverbs 23:7 (NKJV)

Your mind and your thinking are at the core of who you are. Your thoughts are so powerful. Proverbs 23:7 is saying that what you think determines who you are. This is a "selah" moment, which means to stop and ponder on what was said. I need you to get this – you can only get as far as your mind allows you to. If you have a mindset of "I cannot" then you will not and you never will. If you have a poverty mindset, then you will never prosper financially. If by chance you gain wealth, you will lose it quickly if your mindset does not change.

Have you ever heard of people winning millions of dollars and then ending up worse off than they were before? Why does that happen? It is because although they became wealthy, their poverty thinking never changed and as a result, they had no choice but to end up poor again. They went from poverty to riches, then right back to poverty, but this time they are worse off because now they are poor with rich people's problems, such as millions of dollars of debt. But this will not be the case with the children of God. God has given us a spirit of wisdom and we will learn to walk in it.

To better understand the mind and its impact on your future, let us take a step all the way back to Genesis to understand who we are as humans.

Then God said, "Let Us make man in Our image, according to Our likeness; let them have dominion over the fish of the sea, over the birds of the air, and over the cattle, over all the earth and over every creeping thing that creeps on the earth."
Genesis 1:26 (NKJV)

"And the LORD God formed man of the dust of the ground, and breathed into his nostrils the breath of life; and man became a living soul." Genesis 2:7 (NKJV)

This is our beginning and therefore our understanding of it is crucial. First, we see here that God formed mankind. In other words, He created and designed our body. It was a work of art and He was the inspiration. He made us look just like Him, for Scripture teaches that we were made in His image and likeness. To be created in His image means we were designed to look like and resemble Him. We are His reflection, and this is a great honor. Next time you look in the mirror, know that you look good because you look like God. Pause and smile (smiley face inserted here).

To be created in His likeness means that we function the same way He does. We display His character and personality. This is amazing to me and the more I learn about God's character, the more eager I become to display Him in my interactions with others. The truth is, you and I were designed to act and behave just like God. The bolded statement below is very powerful and one that I love to teach.

All along, God intended for the human being to operate and live the same way He does.

I want to point out how Genesis 2 tells us that God Himself formed the human race. So no, you are not something that accidentally evolved from a monkey or gorilla. And no, when you go to the zoo and see the primates, you are not staring at your distant cousins. You are part of God's strategic plan of creation and dominion, and you were made by His hands.

Next, we see that God breathed into man. The lifeless sculpture of mankind laid next to God. He blew air from His mouth into the nostrils of man and this earthly, hand-carved structure suddenly became alive and a living soul.

The Hebrew word for living soul is nephesh (Strong's number 05315)[1] and it involves everything that makes us who we are. As the breath of God entered the human body, mankind rose to life. The spirit of the human was born as well as the will, emotions, life in the blood, soul, character, passions, and mind (taken from the definition of nephesh[2]).

Let us set our attention on the last one listed – the mind. We received our minds when God breathed into us and gave us life. This means that your mind contains the Spirit of God. This is powerful. Your mind is not meant to wander on its own and think whatever drops into it at that moment. God gave you your mind as a piece of Him. Our minds should display the character, power, and ability of God.

Your mind is a part of God that was given to you to position you to be like God.

This was the great deception in the Garden of Eden. satan told Eve that if she ate the fruit she would be just like God – the problem was that she was already just like God (Genesis 1:26 – 28). And so are you, but we must think like God in order to display

His character and power. I love this Scripture (and shout out to my dad as this is his favorite verse):

> *"And Jesus answering said unto them, have faith in God"*
> Mark 11:22 (NKJV)

In Greek, the word "in" also means "like". In Mark 11:22, if you replace the word in with like, Jesus was saying to His disciples, "Have faith like God." If you read the entire phrase in Greek, it reads something like, "have the faith of God." In other words, Jesus expected his disciples to display the same faith God has which allowed Him to create the entire universe by simply speaking it into existence (Genesis 1:3-31). This is another Selah moment for you to pause and digest. This is a part of the "likeness" of God we were created in.

> *"God, who gives life to the dead and calls those things which do not exist as though they did"*
> Romans 4:17 (NKJV)

If we are not using our minds and mouths to create and speak things into existence, then we are not functioning as God intended for us to.

We see that the mind is not a natural object. We think of it as being natural because we tie the mind to the brain, but the mind itself is part of our spirit being and not part of our flesh. Mankind received its mind, or nephesh, not when God formed us from the ground but when He breathed life into us. Our mind was created from the breath of God and is, therefore, part of our spirit being.

I have come to realize that the mind connects the carnal world to the spirit world. The link between the supernatural and the natural is the mind. It is the bridge that allows us to go into the depths of the spirit and causes angels and demons to interact with humans. I repeat, the mind is what allows angels and demons to interact with humans.

Have you ever worshiped God or prayed but were unfocused? You were singing or speaking words, but your mind was distracted by other things and the outcome was probably nothing much. Then suddenly you focus your attention on the worship or prayer and suddenly you make that connection with God. You feel Him and connect with Him more deeply and even receive a breakthrough. What made the difference? You put your mind into it! Once your mind was into the worship or prayer you were offering, you were able to connect your spirit to God and receive your breakthrough. It has happened to me countless times.

Once my mind connects with the activity that my body is doing, then power is created. The ability to achieve and see results is born.

When I was pregnant with my first child, I was afraid of labor. In fact, at one point I used to say that I would not have children because I was afraid to deal with the pain of giving birth. At around seven months of pregnancy, I started dedicating time every day to speak to myself and change my mind about labor. Yes, I decided to change my mind. I convinced myself that labor was easy because I am a woman, and I was born for this (among many other things). My body knows exactly what it is doing and that is how God designed it. I spent forty-five minutes to an hour each day rehearsing these statements and preparing myself for birth. When the time came, I opted for an epidural but due to complications, it did not work. I unwillingly had a somewhat natural birth, and can I tell you that when I left the delivery room I was dancing and felt very empowered! My labor experience was comfortable and it was positive! People are shocked when I tell them this, but why did that happen? It was a mindset shift. I worked diligently to change my thinking, to undo the years of horror stories I was told by many other women, and to tell myself a new story. I forced my mind to accept a new truth - that labor was easy because I was designed for it. My mind believed, and therefore labor was easy.

I am hoping by now you are beginning to understand that your mind is a powerful tool and your diligent attention to the thoughts it thinks is very important. The thoughts that are in your mind are so powerful that they actually go into your future and prepare it for you. This is why someone with a poverty mindset will always be poor. Remember, you cannot go beyond your thoughts. This is precisely what our opening Scripture means – you are what you think or you become what you think.

The mind is so powerful and filled with creative power, making it all the more important that you pay extra close attention to what you allow your mind to think. My rule is, if I do not want that thought to be my reality, then I should stop myself from thinking it.

It is critical to your success and your future to establish a healthy, Godly mindset towards every area of your life. This includes the way you think about yourself and your future, your ability, and even things like your marriage and family, your health, your career and business, and your finances. Through this book, we will focus on the financial aspect of your mindset. You will come face to face with Godly thinking on money and learn God's view of and plan for your finances. We need to shed wrong thinking concerning our finances and establish new ways of thinking about money.

Here are some thoughts I want you to shed:

If God wants me to be rich, then I will get rich.

The truth – many people die with their dreams and destinies still within them, leaving earth never having shared their gifts with the rest of us or reaped any benefits from them. In fact, according to Dr. Myles Munroe, the graveyard is the wealthiest place on earth. In it lies books that were never written, businesses that never got off the ground, songs that were never written or produced, and so many ideas and dreams that never came to fruition.

God has many wonderful plans for you. The Bible says that God knew you before you were ever in your mother's womb (Jeremiah 1:5). God set you apart for your purpose before you were born. His plans for you are so great and grand but if you fail to do your part, they will not happen. This is why the cemetery is so wealthy because it is filled with people who did not do their part and their dreams died with them. Our walk with God is a partnership between us and Him. You must do your part and we will continue to explore this in the remainder of this book.

I will get checks in the mail or some random person will give me millions of dollars and I will be rich.

The truth – While on rare occasions God does bless in these ways, this is not normal, nor should you sit around expecting this to be your means to gain wealth. God is the Miracle Worker who does all sorts of impossible things beyond our comprehension, but if you want wealth, it will not come like "magic," that is, it will not mysteriously appear in your bank account. We have come to expect this hocus pocus type of God and that mindset is demonic. Please understand that I do know that miracles such as checks in the mail and people handing money over to you do happen, but these miracles are not meant to sustain you for a lifetime. They are temporary blessings that last for a season. There is more that has to be done to build wealth, sustain it throughout your future, and leave behind an inheritance for your descendants. God sets high expectations for us. There is a role you play in your future and God loves you too much to let you be lazy while He just hands you wealth on a silver platter. He wants you to do your part so that you can grow and then turn around and help others on the journey.

So, stop waiting to get rich by magic and make your mind up that you will do whatever it is God has for you to do.

Poverty is a sign of humility.

It is not. Poverty is a sign of lack, including the lack of knowledge because knowledge leads to wealth. People can be poor and proud and others can be rich and humble. Let us take a look at this revelation the Holy Spirit gave to me.

> *"Likewise you younger people, submit yourselves to your elders.*
> *Yes, all of you be submissive to one another,*
> *and be clothed with humility, for*

> *'God resists the proud, but gives grace to the humble.'*
> *Therefore humble yourselves under the mighty hand of God,*
> *that He may exalt you in due time"*
> *1 Peter 5:5-6 (NKJV)*

Here we see a sign of humility is the ability to submit to each other, and this is a requirement of all of us who follow Jesus Christ. But it says that God "gives grace to the humble." Grace is in essence a God-like ability to get things done. The Greek word used here is "Charis" which means joy, pleasure, delight, knowledge, affection; but more strongly, it speaks of obtaining divine help, power, and governance. (New Testament Greek Lexicon[3]).

What we see here, is that God gives the humble a divine ability to accomplish more. He helps them accomplish what they cannot do by themselves. This grace spans every area of the lives of the humble – from their spiritual walk with God, to victories all around including their marriage, career, business, parenting, finances, etc. God's plan for the humble is exaltation. Therefore, He gives the humble His own ability to do things they otherwise could not have done, and this leads to their exaltation.

The Holy Spirit then reminded me of Deuteronomy 8:18, which says God has given us the ability to build wealth. This word ability is grace and knowledge. He gives us a special grace, power, and knowledge that enables us to do what we could not have done in our own strength, understanding, and capability. (This is why I can say that poverty is a sign of a lack of knowledge.) According to 1 Peter 5, we see that He gives this amazing grace to the humble. So God gives the humble the power to build wealth and to do anything they need to do.

So if you believe you are humble, you can go before God with this Scripture and ask for the power, the grace, and the knowledge to get wealth. And in fact, there is knowledge right in this book to build wealth.

I have learned a lot about the grace of God through my own experiences. I often take on more than one person can handle, such as working eighty or more hours a week, pursuing a master's degree, writing this book, and starting my own business, all at the same time while being a wife and mom to two toddlers. I accomplish so much more (and the results are more excellent) when I rely on God's grace and not my ability. I saw firsthand how powerful and impactful the grace of God is in our lives. I will do nothing except by His grace.

1 Peter 5 and verse 6 concludes that if we are humble, God will lift us up in due time. This is again because of the grace spoken of in verse 5 – that special ability He gives you in your humbled state

that leads to your exaltation. Get ready for your lifting because it is your turn for elevation.

My family has always been poor.

Your future is not based on your past. In fact, the Bible tells us that God will use the low things of this Earth to confound the wise, that is to confuse and even amaze them.

"For you see your calling, brethren, that not many wise according to the flesh, not many mighty, not many noble, are called. But God has chosen the foolish things of the world to put to shame the wise, and God has chosen the weak things of the world to put to shame the things which are mighty; and the base things of the world and the things which are despised God has chosen, and the things which are not, to bring to nothing the things that are, that no flesh should glory in His Presence."
1 Corinthians 1:26 – 29 (NKJV)

That means God looks for those whom others have rejected, the ones who seemed doomed to fail, doomed to not succeed, or amount to anything. He uses those who are low and base. Why? Because first, He is drawn to those who have a broken spirit and who are humbled. He is drawn to the ones whom society has written off and those that are looked down upon. Those who have the odds stacked up against them, or who are a statistic, according to earthly standards.

Second, God loves to do grand things in the lives of the least qualified so that He gets all the glory. It is a type of "only God can do this." God wants to transform your life so much that those who think they know you so well will not be able to recognize you and all they can say is that it had to have been God. All of this again, speaks to the grace we discussed above.

God is about dramatic transformation. Are you ready to be His next masterpiece?

Here is a statistic that I want you to keep in mind. According to a 2017 survey done by Fidelity Investments, 88% of millionaires are self-made. That means that only 12% of millionaires had their wealth handed down to them. The remaining 88% were "ordinary people" as some might describe them. None of them were born millionaires. You too can become a millionaire regardless of your background or upbringing.

I want to get rich, but I have no idea where to even begin.

Begin to tell yourself that God will show you the way. He already has a plan for your life and He will reveal it if you will come along this journey with Him. God knows where you should begin and He will reveal it to you. In fact, He has already placed it in your heart.

Through this book and the accompanying workbook, we will draw out the dreams God has placed in your heart. Do not let this feeling of being unsure hold you back. If God tells you to open a lemonade stand and all you have are lemons and no water and sugar, then just get started peeling your lemons. As you move forward with what you have, your phone will ring, someone will knock on your door, or God will give you an instruction to go somewhere and you will come into the remaining ingredients.

It is wrong for me to desire money or riches, for the love of money is the root of all evil.

The Bible does teach that the love of money is the root of all kinds of evil but desiring wealth and loving money are two different things. Money needs to have the right place in your heart – you cannot love it nor should it come first. We cover this topic in more detail in the next chapter.

The Bible says,

"...money answers all things." Proverbs 10:19c (NKJV)

"Giving a gift can open doors; it gives access to important people!" Proverbs 18:16 (NLT)

Money opens doors for us. Proverbs 18:16 was written to provide wisdom to God's children but the children of the world have used this to their advantage more so than the children of God. Many wealthy people are making donations to organizations and community leaders and in turn, push their influence. God wants His children with His values elevated to positions of influence and Proverbs 18 tells us money opens that door. It grants us access to decision-makers and allows us to influence those decisions using Godly principles and values.

This is why your ideas and your dreams matter – because you will bring Jesus to a world or sector where He is desperately needed.

It is a deception of the enemy that God does not want you rich or that you should not desire or pray about money. God wants you to have it all, as far as your eyes can see is what He told Abraham.

"For all the land which you see I give to you and your descendants [seed] forever" Genesis 13:15. (NKJV).

We are the seed of Abraham and the promise is for us.

"And if you are Christ's, then you are Abraham's seed, and heirs according to the promise." Galatians 3:29 (NKJV).

The promise God made Abraham was for abundant wealth, including businesses (his herds, camels, livestock, etc.) Do not be afraid to embrace prosperity and the idea of you becoming wealthy. As a student of the Word of God, I understand that the promise of Abraham is not all financial – it encompasses all forms of prosperity including salvation through Jesus Christ, which is part of soul prosperity. However, we need to stop ignoring the financial prosperity aspect of the promise. We see clearly that God promised wealth to Abraham and He fulfilled that promise. Abraham made it known that it was God who gave him riches – if God did that for Abraham, why not you? Aren't you a Child of God? Your Daddy wants you to prosper too!

God wants you to prosper so believe it now. Pray for your prosperity and desire it. John prayed for us to prosper in 3 John 2, so therefore you can go ahead and pray for prosperity.

> *"Beloved, I pray that you may **prosper in all things** and be in health, just as your soul prospers." 3 John 2 (NKJV)*

The prosperity of your soul is critical, but God does not stop there. He says He wishes we "prosper in all things." What do "all things" mean to you? God leaves nothing out. In **everything** you do, God wants you to prosper, and your finances are no exception.

It will never happen for me. I just don't have what it takes.

This is so not true. God gives us the wisdom that we need to make wealth. As we saw above, Deuteronomy chapter 8 and verse 18 tells us that God gives us the ability to gain wealth so that He keeps His covenant with us. He actually made a covenant to make us wealthy and He wants to keep His Word. Blessing you to get rich is one of the ways God keeps His Word. This is another selah (or maybe shouting) moment.

> *"And you shall remember the Lord your God, for it is He who gives you power to get wealth, that He may establish His covenant which He swore to your fathers, as it is this day."*
> *Deuteronomy 8:18 (NKJV)*

In the Scripture above the word, "fathers" refer to our forefathers Abraham, Isaac, and Jacob. God made a promise to them to make us wealthy. As we saw earlier from Galatians 3, if we believe in Christ, then we are the children of Abraham. He is our forefather, so the promise of wealth is for us as well. Abraham is the father of faith, so I just want to point out that it is not just a promise of wealth, but all the promises that come with faith in Jesus Christ, including salvation, victory in every area of our lives, and ultimately eternal life in Heaven.

Make up your mind that from this moment, you will not allow these negative thoughts and others like them to float around in your mind. You are taking control of your mind and your life and will stop believing the lies the enemy has told you. Affirm positive things concerning your future and your finances and have a healthy, Godly mindset towards your money and prosperity.

Here are some positive, new thoughts you can adopt:

- It is the will of God that I prosper.

- God wants to bless me so that I can be a blessing to others.

- God is the One who gives me the ability to gain wealth. I can pray and ask Him for this ability and He will give it to me. He gets all the praise and glory.
- God made a covenant to bless those who believe in Him and in prospering me, He is keeping His Word.

- My success and prosperity bring glory to God.

- My success and prosperity will help advance the Kingdom of God.
- I am ready to make wealth and God will guide me every step of the way.

- My desires are not wrong – God wants me to have the good of the land, just as He spoke through the prophet Isaiah. He wants me to have the best of everything.

- I want to be rich. I will be rich and there is nothing wrong with thinking like this.

To dig further into your mindset and the shift you need to make, go to the Workbook that accompanies this book and complete chapter 1 exercises.

CHAPTER 2

A Love Affair

"No one can serve two masters. Either you will hate the one and love the other, or you will be devoted to the one and despise the other. You cannot serve both God and money."
Matthew 6:24 (NIV)

It's enticing; it's luring. It calls to you with desire, saying
"Pleasures are in my hand, to you I will give grandeur.
Eat my fruit at any cost and the world will be yours.
Drink of my drink and your desires come to reality.
I am the answer to it all.
The friend of the great, the leader of the stars.
I call and they answer, they do as I tell them.
Their reward is in my hand, the world I give to them."
But be wise.
To eat its fruit is delicious but to love it is death.

Money is a hot topic in society and the Church. As my poem above states, it possesses the ability to give wealth, luxury, and make many dreams come true. However, the place money has in our hearts is very important to understand. We want to be people who are wisely able to build wealth and use it to further the Kingdom of God, our lives, and the lives of our loved ones, but we do not want to fall into the trap of loving money. As the poem says, we can enjoy the fruit it gives but the love of money leads to dangerous evils.

> *"For the love of money is the root of all kinds of evil.*
> *Some people, eager for money, have wandered from the faith and*
> *pierced themselves with many griefs."*
> *1 Timothy 6:10 (NIV)*

Many have incorrectly quoted 1 Timothy 6:10 as reading money is the root of all evil. What the Scripture actually says is the *love* of money is the root of all kinds of evil. Emphasis should be placed on the word love. We see this in society today when people set aside their moral values to gain money. Bribes, deception, murder, jealousy, and envy are just some of the evils that the love of money has brought into society. According to I Timothy 6, money is not the issue nor is it the focus of this Scripture. The place money has in our hearts is the real issue.

God never commanded us to love money; He commands us to love Him and to love each other. Loving money is against the will of God and therefore is sinful. To love money is to lust after it. You become a servant to it, making money your master. If you love money, you obey the call to gain money over fulfilling the will, purposes, and intents of God: but this is the great deception of money. The truth is, when you chase after the will of God to bring about His purposes, money and provision will naturally follow. Provision follows purpose.

Before we move on, let us understand one thing. The love of money is not simply a concept. It is a stronghold of the mind. It can also be referred to as the lust for money. The lust for money or the strong desire for money can lead someone to the point of putting financial increase above their relationship with God and family, and money then becomes an addiction. The lust for money puts someone under the illusion that money is above everything and will satisfy all their needs. This is an evil mental influence and a powerful deception.

Many today have all the riches they desire, yet they have lost their health, their marriage, and their relationship with their family. The love of money can seem pleasurable and rewarding at first but leads to a miserable end; an end the enemy of your soul desires for you. Is not loving money, after all, a demonic stronghold? Many need to be delivered from the demonic stronghold of loving or lusting after money.

For everything in the world – the lust of the flesh, the lust of the eyes, and the pride of life – does not come from the Father but from the world. 1 John 2:16 (NKJV).

Is not lusting after money led by the lust of the flesh, the lust of the eyes, and the pride of life? The lust for money is to please the fleshly needs, to look good and have things that look good, and obtain a high stature in the sight of others. This also reveals that lusting for money is rooted in pride. It is self-seeking which is against the character of The Father, who exemplifies humility and love. This is the kind of love that instructs us to meet the needs of others (1 Corinthians 13:4).

As you continue reading this book, you will see that God does want you to have the best of the best. Of course, God wants you to be wealthy and financially prosperous. The point I want you to see here is in your desire and pursuit. Desire God and pursue His will for your life. Even as you build wealth, your heart is not chasing wealth but instead, your focus is on fulfilling the will of God for your life. Do not lust after money and do not make it your number one priority. When you chase God, riches will chase you. In other words, provision is in abundant supply in the Kingdom of our Heavenly Father and as you follow Him, He will unveil them to you. We will discuss this in more detail as we progress through the book.

The spirit of loving money is indeed at the root of much of the evil we see in the world today. People go to various extremes just to make money. Some even sell their souls to the devil because money means that much to them. The problem with this is that the soul is exceedingly more valuable than money and anything money can supply. To sell one's soul for money is like trading in the most expensive diamond in the world for a handful of cement, yet the soul is not even comparable in worth to the most expensive diamond in the world. The soul is very powerful and gives us our God-like qualities. No amount of money in the world is worth your soul.

In this chapter, I want you to check your heart. Ask the Holy Spirit to search your heart and reveal any area where the love of money may be. Open your heart to Him and be attentive (very attentive) and receptive to what He shows you.

Below are some examples of how the love of money operates:

1. Companies are dishonest about their products to generate more sales.

2. Someone murders a loved one to get life insurance money.

3. A leader accepts a bribe and acts illegally or dishonestly.

4. Making decisions solely based on money versus seeking the counsel of God to find out His will.

5. A Christian singer or speaker will only minister at events that can pay them a high fee, versus ministering where God leads them to, even if it means doing so for free.

6. A person who is able to and has the opportunity to give to charity and the needy, but constantly refuses to.

7. Not wanting to be separate from your money, including a fear of investing, giving money away, or tithing.

8. Jealous of what someone else has financially or materially and hating them in your heart or planning evil against them.

As believers in Jesus Christ, we live according to His will. He has a plan for all of us and we must find out what that plan is and live accordingly. When we allow money to lead in our decision-making, we have bowed to it as lord.

For example, a minister is invited to speak at two locations on the same date. He must choose one as he cannot be in both places at once. If he decides to go with the option that pays the most simply because of the additional cash, then money is the lord of his life. He obeyed the "voice" of money and essentially went with the option money told him to go with. If Jesus is his Lord, then he would have prayed and found out where God wanted him to go and would have followed that path. Maybe God still would have sent him to the higher-paying option but by seeking and following God's will, this minister was not allowing money to rule over him. In his heart, he was motivated by his love for God and his willingness to minister to God's people. He was not motivated by the amount of money he would make. In this same scenario, if God tells the minister to attend the event that paid less (or one that did not even pay at all) and he obeyed, then his love for God is above his desire for money because he obeyed God even when it meant he would receive less money.

The opening verse, Matthew 6:24, makes it clear – you cannot love both God and money. There is only one throne in the heart of a human being and that throne must be reserved for God. Two gods cannot sit on that throne. One will have to give up the throne if another arrives.

When we love money, we impeach God from His throne in our hearts and we give money His place.

Money takes rule and our decisions are based on money and not on the will of God. When this happens, evil can easily take over our lives as we begin to compromise to make more money. Small compromises then lead to larger compromises.

The Role of Money

I am excited for you to get into the next chapter to understand God's perspective on money. Right now, let us be sure we know the role of money in our lives, as God intended. Keep this in mind – **money should not be lord over you, instead, you should rule over it.**

As a human being, you have been given dominion over everything on the earth to rule over it and this includes money and wealth. You control your finances and it should not control you. You are a king or queen over your life and resources, and you should reign over your finances. I want to teach you how to rule over your money well and thereby increase it and no devil in hell can stop you.

Please understand the following:

1. Money is meant to advance your life so you, your family, and your community can be blessed by your wealth. God wants us to have the best. He said that if we would follow

His instructions, we would eat the good of the land (Isaiah 1:19). God wants you to have more than what you have. The increase you daydream about and wish you had, is nothing compared to the increase God desires for you. He wants more wealth for you than you want for yourself, and I will teach you in this book how to become wealthy God's way.

2. Money is meant to advance the Kingdom. Have you noticed who is advancing in society? The most influential people are wealthy people. Could you imagine if executives of the largest companies, politicians, lawmakers, celebrities, entertainers, etc. were all people who loved and served God and people who lived righteously and obeyed God's Word? Our society would be much different. When God's people are wealthy, they are more influential in the world, and therefore are able to bring Godly standards to the arena they operate in. Our society, laws, schools, companies, television programs, culture, music, entertainment, sports, etc. will reflect Godly principles. This is what God desires. This establishes His rule in our world. How deeply can we impact society at large with God's standards when a majority of the church is poor, broke, just getting by, and barely surviving? As we learned in chapter 1, money opens doors to put those who hold it in the face of decision-

makers and culture shifters. If more Christians had wealth, then more of the decisions made and more of our values and culture as a society would reflect our Godly standards.

3. Money helps us take care of each other. It is at the heart of God that we love one another. Jesus said this is the way the world will know that we are His disciples (John 13:35). It is our love for one another that sets us apart from the world. I have learned that when God blesses one, it is meant for others also. For example, Tara is praying for God to provide her with a car. Lisa gets a significant pay increase and wants to give herself a luxury car as a reward. God tells Lisa to buy two cars – one for her and one for Tara. If Lisa is attentive to God's voice and her heart loves Him, she will obey. Tara has received her blessing, not by God giving her a car directly, but by Lisa obeying and giving Tara a car. What Lisa needs to understand is that when God gave her the financial increase, He calculated Tara's car into it. It is not Lisa's money because all that we have belong to God – He gave her the money to meet her needs and the needs of Tara. Scripture says,

> *"But whoever has this world's goods, and sees his brother in need, and shuts up his heart from him, how does the love of God abide in him?" 1 John 3:17 (NKJV)*

Loving God means we take care of the material and financial needs of each other. Well, how can we do so if we are only making enough money to just get by? Your financial increase means that you have more to give to those in the Kingdom of God who are in need and this is one of the reasons why God wants you to be rich. There are others whose blessings are tied up in your prosperity, like Tara in the example above. As we read earlier, God told Abraham that He will bless him so he can be a blessing to others.

When God increases you, He is factoring in the needs of your community. Your community is those whom God has placed in your sphere of influence. It includes some of your family members, people in your neighborhood and your local church, certain charities, and even people all around the world that He will place on your heart and in your path to bless.

One of our son's favorite bedtime stories is The Good Samaritan. Jesus taught this story to explain who our neighbors are, what I refer to as your community. It is a popular Bible story of a man who was beaten, robbed, and left on the street helpless. The priest and temple worker walks by and offers him no help. In fact, the priest pretends he did not see the man hurt and wounded.

How many times do we close our ears and eyes to the needs of others, simply because we do not want the responsibility or to be bothered?

Later, a Samaritan man is walking down the road and sees the man lying on the street. He picks him up and bandages his wounds. He gets him water to drink. He then places the man on his donkey and takes him to an inn. He spends the night at the inn caring for the man. The next morning, he not only pays for the night's stay, but he pays in advance for the hurt man to continue to remain at the inn until he gets better. He lets the owner of the inn know that if the bill is higher than what he has prepaid, he will pay the additional cost on his journey back.

An important note to make here is that the wounded man was a Jew, and Jews and Samaritans were enemies. Jews looked down upon Samaritans because they were mixed-race and not purely Jewish. I believe Jesus used a Samaritan in this story for a reason. He was making it known that in this new "religion" he is establishing, there is no room for racial inequities. The one you think is least among you is the one He selects to display His heart and purpose on the Earth. The good Samaritan did not let the racial divide and hatred stop him from helping this Jewish man. He acted in love.

If you were to dig deep in your heart, would you do the same thing? Would you love to that degree? The Samaritan man changed his plans and went out of his way to help someone who looked down on him and probably hated him. Would you do the same for an enemy?

Another item to note is the Samaritan had to have been able to afford all of this. If he was broke, no matter how much his heart wanted to act in love and help, his poverty would have limited his ability to do so. As God increases you, increase your blessings to those you come in contact with. Your community needs you and there are specific people God has placed within your community. You are an answer to their prayer; you are the one God wants to use to help them, so be prepared. Your wealth will end the sufferings of many and the more you give, the more God will ensure you always have plenty to give. He sees that He can trust you and therefore will continue to increase you more and more.

As an example, my community includes several boys and girls rescued from sex trafficking because I donate to charities that fight to save their lives; the people in various parts of Africa who only had access to dirty, disease-ridden water but now have access to clean water wells due to the hard work of charities I (and many others) donate to; the neighbor whose husband left her and is struggling financially; the friend at church who needed some financial help and asked for a loan but instead received a gift.

These are examples to show you what your community can consist of.

Being a cheerful giver is a great way to overcome the love of money. It displays God's hand on the Earth as we take care of the needs of one another.

Please refer to the Workbook, chapter 2 for soul searching exercises and prayers to help you discover and deal with the love of money in your life.

CHAPTER 3

Know Your God

"...but the people that know their God shall be strong and carry out great exploits."
Daniel 11:32b (NKJV)

I love Daniel 11:32. It resonates with me and empowers me every time I read it. Why don't you read this verse to yourself at least five times and let it get into your heart? If we know our God, not only will our strength increase but there is no limit to what we can do. There are so many great things God has planned for you to do. Long before you were born, He mapped out your destiny and designed your purpose.

> *"Before I formed you in the womb I knew you,*
> *before you were born I set you apart..."*
> *Jeremiah 1:5 (NIV)*

Let us see the beautiful revelation in this verse. God is speaking to the prophet Jeremiah and tells him that before he was formed in the womb, God already knew him. That is interesting. Before he was ever in his mother's womb God already knew him and called him to be a prophet to the nations. Do you see it? That must mean Jeremiah existed before he entered his mother's womb. He was on God's mind all along. The same is true for you. God knew you long before you were ever a thought in your parents' minds. It does not matter what method was used to bring you here – some came in a loving home with mother and father while some may not even know their birth parents. There are even those who came through rape. No one should feel condemned because of how they came here. The point is you are here and your life was ordained by God.

But as many as received Him, to them He gave the right to become children of God, to those who believe in His name: who were born, not of blood, nor of the will of the flesh, nor of the will of man, but of God. John 1:12-13 (NKJV)

The Scripture above brings so much hope to those who feel unhappy with their birth or ashamed. It says that when you believe in Jesus, your natural birth is erased, and all God sees is that you were born from Him. The NIV says you are not born of "natural descent" or of any "human decision" – you descended from God Himself. I personally know someone who was born through rape.

This person became the first to get saved in his family and since then has led hundreds, if not thousands, to the Lord.

I want you to hear the heart of God as it was expressed in John 1:12 and 13. You were never an accident. Before you ever entered your mother's womb, you existed and were known by God. He knew you and designed you for His will and placed you in the womb of your mother. In His plan, this was the family and the mother he wanted to use to usher you into the earth realm, just like Mary was the woman He used to bring Jesus to earth. Your family might have been dysfunctional but every trial you endured and every hardship you suffered will work together perfectly in God's plan to make you an even better version of yourself.

Not everything you went through was of God. The evil in the world today tearing apart lives and families are from the devil and people who chose to disobey God. But even the storms the devil threw your way to try to take you out, if you will trust God with it all, they will work for your good if you love God (Romans 8:28).

I recall the testimony of one woman whom I love dearly and look up to. She was severely raped and molested several times. Had the man who harmed her been obedient to God, he would have never done this. As I mentioned earlier, evil comes from the devil and people who chose to follow his suggestions and disobey God. This evil could have destroyed her if the devil had his way,

BUT GOD! God took a hold of her and walked her through a healing journey, and today she is not only free from that past, but she is helping both men and women who have suffered rape and molestation to find their freedom. Because of her past, God is using her to help so many others find freedom.

This is a great example of God making all things work for our good. Not only will you come out of the fiery furnace and not even smell like smoke, but you will also help others as well because you have traveled the road they are traveling and you know the way out.

Your victory is certain, nothing is surer, and when you have tasted the other side, you will lead others to their victory and show them the way.

Know your God. Know how He formed you. You are not *just a human*. You are filled with His Spirit and your ability is limitless because He is your God. You are precious to Him. He did not just form you to go through life blindly, with no purpose and achievements. You were not meant to do what I call "follow the herd" – wake up, go to work, work all day, come home, tend to your home, go to sleep to wake up and do it all over again – following the masses and masses of people who are just living a life following the pattern that someone else created. God's plan will break you free from that pattern and set you up for your destiny, so you are living life with purpose. There is much more to you than you can imagine. You are called to influence and to bring change. You are called to set standards and not just follow the herd.

Let us look at the story of Moses and the Exodus. If you are not familiar with the story, you can read it beginning at Exodus chapter 1. The Israelites were in slavery to the Egyptians for four hundred years and they cried out to God for deliverance. God sent Moses to be His Hand on the Earth and set them free, but God had a strategy. He always has a plan and He looks for us to trust Him every step of the way. God does not reveal all the details of His plan. He gives them to us in pieces. This has caused many to stumble because they do not understand what God is doing and therefore, they choose to abort the mission. This is a lack of faith. We must trust Him even when things are not clear to us. We hold onto His Hand as dear children and trust Him to lead us every step of the way. God did not want to just deliver the Israelites from slavery. He had two clear goals in mind:

1. To show the world His might and power so all people would honor both Him and the Israelites since He was their God.

2. Make the Israelites extremely wealthy (the promised land).

God came up with a plan on how to accomplish this and that plan included the ten plagues. You see, by those plagues, God revealed who He was. He showed through each plague that He controlled the sky, the water, the air, the earth, the animals, the human body, the weather, and every other aspect of our human world. He showed Himself as the One and Only Omnipotent God; the only One Sovereign over all else. Selah.

Long before the ten plagues were over, the Egyptians were ready for the Israelites to get out of their land. They were begging Pharaoh to set the Israelites free because they could not take the demonstrations of God anymore. This is what God wanted – for all to see they are no match for Him. None is equal to Him, and none can contend with Him and win.

This is the heart of God for you as well. He will defend you at all costs. He will fight for you with mighty demonstrations. When the enemy rises against you, they are truly rising against God. You are His child and therefore an enemy of yours makes themselves an enemy of Him. Think of this in the natural with your children, whether current or future. If someone harms your child, how will you react? How will you feel? Parents go to great lengths to protect and defend their children. If you hate my child, you automatically hate me because my child is of me. We are one. By harming the children of Israel, Pharaoh made himself an enemy of God.

I do feel the need to make a statement on behalf of those who are from Egypt today. God does not hate or dislike Egyptians and you are not an enemy. Back in that time, the Egyptians held the Israelites as slaves and the story depicts their freedom from slavery. As the Old Testament is a shadow of things to come (Colossians 2:17), this entire story is correctly interpreted as a spiritual enemy. Today, the Church speaks of Egypt as a representation of bondage. Pharaoh and the Egyptians in the story are a representation of demonic activity and anything holding us back. It is not about the actual people of Egypt. The people of Egypt are equally loved by Jesus Christ. I just had to clarify in the event that someone from Egypt is reading this, they do not feel down.

So, what are your enemies? What are the things working against you? Are they generational curses, battles in your mind, hidden sins, and issues in your heart, demonic attacks, lack of progress, stagnation, sickness, low self-esteem, poverty, etc.? There are even people who may be working against you. Nothing that comes against you is a match for your God. If you cry out to Him as the Israelites did, He is sure to rescue you. You are important to Him and with a mighty hand of power He will do whatever you need Him to do for you.

The entire nation of Egypt was destroyed when God was through with them. God took down an entire nation – the economy fell, agriculture was destroyed, and the country was in ruins. But He did not stop there. He was so in love with His people that He wanted them to have the best. He decided to give them the land of the Canaanites, Hittites, Amorites, Perizzites, Hivites, and Jebusites. A land He described as flowing with milk and honey. It was the best of the best – the best houses, the best businesses, the greatest wealth, the best of everything. He wanted them to have it because of His love for them. He loved them with no restraint and nothing can stop God when He is on a mission. No one can dare get in His way, but if one dares, like Pharaoh and his army, they will drown in their defeat. By the end of the Exodus story, we see that God took down multiple nations and kingdoms and handed them over to the Israelites. Not just one nation, but many fell so that God could bless His people in a colossal way.

I am hoping by now your heart is stirring with excitement, and that you see how much He loves you and wants to bless you. He wants you to prosper more than you want to prosper. I recall years ago dreaming of the type of house I wanted to live in. I was coming up with a financial plan to be able to afford this dream house. My husband then told me about a neighborhood he visited that had homes that were beyond impressive. I started looking at them online and right away I thought, "these are way too expensive and even more out of my league than my dream home. Let me not bother looking at these houses and stick to my original plan." Then I felt God stirring in my heart saying, "Why? Why not want more?" I was not expecting that response and to be honest, I was not expecting a response from God at all.

What God started to show me is that I think my dreams are big, but He has even bigger dreams for me. He wanted me to want more. The same is true for you - God wants you to want more. I pray right now that your heart is stirring with dreams and goals for your future.

At the beginning of the Exodus story when God called Moses, He made this promise:

"And I will give this people favor in the sight of the Egyptians; and it shall be, when you go, that you shall not go empty-handed. But every woman shall ask of her neighbor, namely, of her who dwells near her house, articles of silver, articles of gold, and clothing; and you shall put them on your sons and on your daughters. So you shall plunder the Egyptians."
Exodus 3:21-22 (NKJV)

This is a powerful part of the story I do not want us to miss. This was later fulfilled in Exodus 12:36.

"And the LORD gave the people such favor in the sight of the Egyptians that they granted their request. In this way they plundered the Egyptians." (BSB)

God told the Israelites to go to the Egyptians, those who ruled over them, and ask them for their gold and silver as well as their fine linen. The Egyptians were so fearful of the Israelites at the end of the ten plagues, that they literally handed their wealth and riches over to the Israelites and begged them to leave Egypt.

The Israelites became wealthy overnight, but God was working all along in the background. The entire process was not an overnight process. They endured hardship and trials and waited through the ten plagues while God dealt with their enemies.

Although the Bible does not say, Jewish tradition holds that the ten plagues occurred in roughly the course of a year. Some estimate it was only a few months. Nonetheless, God was working on their behalf even when they had no idea and their patience and obedience paid off.

I imagine they were afraid to ask the Egyptians for their wealth. They feared the Egyptians since they ruled over them harshly, but they obeyed God and **their obedience opened the door to bless them with wealth in one night.**

Please refer to the workbook exercise in chapter 3. There you will find an exercise I love to walk people through when I teach on destiny and dreams. It will help you uncover your dreams and face them as well as anything hindering you from them. Have fun!

CHAPTER 4

Breaking the Curse of Poverty

"But Moses told the people, 'Don't be afraid. Just stand still and watch the LORD rescue you today. The Egyptians you see today will never be seen again.'" Exodus 14:13 (NLT)

In the same manner God dealt with the enemies of the Israelites, He wants to deal with your enemies. There may be some things in your life that you need to be delivered from before you can come into wealth. If the Israelites became wealthy in the land of Egypt, they would have lost their wealth to the Egyptians. As the dominant race and the lords over the Israelites, they would have had control over any wealth and riches the Israelites came into. God could not have blessed them in their current position because they needed to be delivered from slavery.

For many of you reading this book, God cannot bless you in the abundant way He would like to as long as you remain in your current position. You cannot get wealthy while you are still in Egypt under the hand of Pharaoh. You need to be delivered from your Egypt first otherwise when His blessings flow into your hands, those same enemies will have it flow right out.

How do the enemies of your finances show up? In many different ways. People who struggle with lack, poverty, or financial bondage seem to not progress financially. Even if they appear to progress, they do not go very far or what they receive is taken away. Most of us have been there or know someone who has been there – each time a financial increase comes to them, the car suddenly needs to get fixed or something else goes wrong that takes the money away from them. This is demonic. What the Bible calls a devourer, is eating away at their finances.

Many people expected to be further in life financially. You are disappointed in where you are but go easy on yourself. Oftentimes, there is a spiritual force working against you. We need to break this power over your life before you can see financial progress. These powers cause money to disappear from the hands of people so their finances never grow past a certain point. Even if their income grows, there is a ceiling placed on their savings, so they are stuck in one place and cannot go past that ceiling. It does not make sense in the natural because it is a spiritual force, and it drives many to frustration and disappointment.

Ask God to begin to reveal to you anything in your life that is not of Him. Ask Him to show you any hindrances blocking your destiny and blessings.

Here are some below but this is not a comprehensive list:

- Fear
- Love of money
- Poverty / lack
- Stagnation; feeling stuck; difficulty progressing
- An inability to save money past a certain point, no matter what your income is; whenever you receive money, it often goes away from you
- Laziness
- Starting but not finishing
- Procrastination
- Feeling often that you are an idiot, less than, or foolish
- Confusion
- Heaviness
- Indecision
- Getting knocked back each time you take a step forward
- Dreams of being in a childhood place or an old place (e.g. the house you grew up in, an old school, etc.). It is a sign

that an enemy of stagnation is trying to keep you from progressing.
- Wrong mindsets, some listed below:
    - "It's too hard"
    - "That's too much"
    - "What's wrong with me?"
    - "I can't do anything right"
    - "I always mess up"
    - "I have bad luck"
    - "I'll never succeed"
    - "I could never do anything great"
    - Thinking you are not as good as everyone else
    - Looking down on yourself
    - Pride – thinking too highly of yourself; thinking you are better than others; looking down on other people; not needing God or thinking you have what it takes all by yourself.

"And from the days of John the Baptist until now the Kingdom of Heaven suffers violence, and the violent take it by force."
Matthew 11:12 (NKJV)

Those who take the Kingdom and get to reap its benefits must take it by force. The Bible teaches us that there is a war going on – a spiritual war. Those who are spiritually violent will fight until they receive their victory. Do you want your piece of the

Kingdom? It will not be handed to you on a silver platter. If you want the Kingdom, then you must grab hold of it and do so with force and power.

The Bible makes it clear that our war is not with people but with the powers of darkness seeking daily to attack our lives.

> *"For we wrestle not against flesh and blood, but against principalities, against powers, against the rulers of the darkness of this world, against spiritual wickedness in high places."*
> *Ephesians 6:12 (NKJV)*

Prior to verse 12, Paul was warning the church to put on the whole armor of God so they would be able to withstand the craftiness of the devil. He deceives by using tricks and tactics that appeal to our desires and emotions in the flesh. He makes things seem true and good when they are sinful and evil. To be honest, this is the reason why I cannot watch television – all I see is the deception of the enemy in movies, sitcoms, shows, etc. Satanic seeds are planted in the minds of the unsuspecting covered with humor, drama, romance, good feelings, etc.

These seeds take root in our minds and produce a harvest that reflects the values of the kingdom of satan. These same seeds also wage war against the seeds God planted inside of us. The Bible calls them thorns and their purpose is to choke the seeds of God and prevent them from growing and bearing fruit. The seeds of God in us are our purpose, destiny, and His Word.

I am not saying you should not watch TV, but I am suggesting that you take caution with what you allow to enter you. What goes in you shapes your thinking and values and ultimately, your behavior. Many of you had dreams of becoming something great until someone planted a seed in you that said you could not. It could have been a teacher or a parent or even an aspect of your culture that shaped your thinking against the seed God placed inside of you. So many things around you war against your seed, that is, your destiny. The enemy will use anything and anyone he can find to stop and to block you. This is why we should always see people and situations through spiritual lenses. Our battle is not with them, but with the invisible enemy of our souls.

In Ephesians 6:12, we are instructed to not only fight the direct demons attacking our lives, communities, and families but to fight against all the leadership in the kingdom of darkness, including the devil himself. Remember, the devil is no match for God. We tend to think of him as being on the same playing field as God. We think of *God versus the devil,* but this is incorrect. There is no God versus anything or anyone. He has no rival and no contender. The devil is at the same level as angels. He is an angel created by God but because of pride, he rebelled against God. He is under God and under our Lord Jesus Christ. We are in Christ and that places us above the devil. You are above lucifer and all his armies of demons. You can win each time you fight if you let the Holy Spirit lead you.

In some cases, we see poverty as a principality that rules over regions and neighborhoods. They sit over poor neighborhoods to keep the people bound. Principalities also establish principles that people, communities, and even entire nations live by. For example, children from a neighborhood who believe that college is not for them – due to their race, economic status, and family background – and as such, they forfeit an opportunity to break a generational curse and do something great. This mindset over an entire community is driven by a principality ruling over that region.

Powers of poverty come from demonic spirits that enter people and can travel through bloodlines, more commonly known as generational curses. These powers hold people trapped with spiritual yokes, chains, ropes, shackles, and mindsets that keep them poor. They can also operate externally, where they are not inside the human body but still have a strong influence over people by making suggestions through their thoughts. For some, it can be difficult to break the hold of these powers over their lives, especially if they are generational. But with God you are victorious. The devil will regret that he ever messed with you!

When I pray prayers of deliverance, there are a few things I always tackle. First strongholds. Strongholds are thoughts the enemy planted in our minds. By choosing to continue thinking about negative and sinful thoughts, we water them and allow them to grow and take root in our lives. A stronghold is a way of thinking. If someone is constantly lusting in their heart, then there is a stronghold of lust there. If someone is constantly thinking about divorcing their spouse, then there could be a stronghold of divorce. Simply put, we make demons comfortable in our minds when we think thoughts that are against God's will, and they get so comfortable that they build a house in our minds and stay there – that is a stronghold.

Secondly, I deal with yokes. A yoke is a strong rope or wooden harness that is placed around the neck of an animal so that its owner can pull it in the direction he or she wants it to go. If the animal resists, a stronger force is used to control it. If you have ever committed a sin you did not want to commit, especially if you have repeated it, then that could be a sign of a yoke of bondage. Many people are bound by a yoke of anger. They lose their temper and it is almost as if they are not aware of how it happened. Something upsets them, and they feel the anger rise inside them and they react. This is a demonic attack and you can resist the devil by using God's Word. We give thanks to God who delivers us with ease through Jesus Christ. No bondage is too strong for

God – you might as well believe you are already delivered because your freedom is certain.

Thirdly, I break satanic covenants and contracts. We may have inadvertently entered into a contract with the devil through disobedience, however, contracts with darkness were typically formed by our ancestors. Spirits are territorial and will remain in a family line until they are kicked out by someone operating under the power of Jesus Christ. These covenants are binding in the spirit realm and give demons a right to operate in the affected person's life and to keep their family in bondage. Everything, however, is subject to our Lord Jesus Christ and no power is greater than Him. In His Name, we can destroy all satanic covenants, even if they were formed hundreds of years ago by our ancestors.

Remember how I said the family you were born into, no matter how bad your upbringing was, was chosen by God? You were sent to be a type of Moses and Joshua to free their bloodline. For some of you, you were raised under negative circumstances such as poverty, anger, alcoholism, and even abuse. Well, God is calling you to freedom so these demonic patterns do not continue in your family line and the next generation can live in freedom. God sent you to deliver them. Your next generation does not have to journey to the promised land like you have to - they will be born in it or arrive when you do. Your freedom, your change, and building the life of your dreams are not just for you, but also for the generations already inside of you that will come from you.

Why are we discussing demons and warfare in a book on prosperity? Well, to have lasting solutions we must deal with the root of our problems. If you only deal with the symptoms, then you will continue to have the symptoms. If you correctly address your problems from the root, then you destroy the source, and only then are you free.

Poverty is not just being poor. God showed me several years ago that I needed to be delivered from a spirit of poverty. It shocked me because I thought I was successful and doing well financially. What He showed me is that I still was not where I should have been in terms of my finances. Although I was prospering by my definition, there was still a spirit of poverty holding me back from the abundance God had planned for me. I was not investing or saving like I should have been, I was spending too much, and there were risks I should have taken to build more wealth that I was too afraid to step out and do. God also revealed to me that while I think my income is great, by this time in my life He planned for me to have a higher income. There were spiritual forces holding my finances back and fear stopped me from making bold moves that would have radically changed my financial status.

This is why the Holy Spirit is upon me to write so passionately in this book – I have been where you are, I have fought the battles you are fighting and experienced the emotions, disappointments, frustrations, etc. you are going through. But now I can say, let me show you the way out.

For some, poverty is a mental stronghold – a mindset that needs to be changed. For others, it is a principality that rules over their neighborhood and they need to break free from its rule. Then there are those to whom poverty is a generational curse and satanic covenant that came from an ancestor, which is evident by poverty in different generations of their family. And yet for others, it is a power and demonic spirit that strategically brings situations into their lives to take away any increase they receive, ensuring they never prosper. Still, for some poverty comes as a lack of sufficient progress – they are not where they should be in life. Whatever it may be, it all comes from the devil and in Jesus Christ, we have the power to stop the enemy and break every curse. We have the power to destroy his plans and take back everything he stole from us.

The devil has delayed you for too long. He has kept you back from your dreams and destiny for far too long. You must stop him. If you do not, the pattern can continue and your children will suffer the same thing you suffered until someone stops him. The devil wants to deceive you with fear and a lack of faith. Will you let him continue, or will you fight back and shut him up? This is not just for you, it is for your children and grandchildren, and all generations that will come from you. Don't you want to take back all that he took from you? Don't you want to finally be in the place that you ought to be? God has strategically chosen you to be the one to set your family free. This is your time.

So, are you ready to fight? Are you ready to get violent?

Find a quiet, private place where you can pray. Let us walk together and break every curse from your life and destroy every chain. Freedom is part of our salvation package in Jesus Christ and the spiritually violent will have it and enjoy it.

Please note, it is important to pray with faith, focus, power, and energy. Pray with all your might and pray like you believe you have what you are saying. James 5:16 reads,

"The effectual fervent prayer of a righteous man availeth much."
(KJV)

Also, Mark 11:24 states,

"Therefore I say to you, whatever things you ask when you pray, believe that you receive them, and you will have them." (NKJV)

Prayer

Lord Jesus, I want Your plans to be fulfilled in my life. Please make me the person You designed me to be. Remove everything in my life that is contrary to You and make me what You desire. I surrender my life to You. Please forgive all my sin and fill me with Your Presence.

Lord Jesus, I recognize that You have a bigger plan for my life than I can imagine. I have decided that I want all that You have for me. I recognize that there may be some demonic activities in my life that have hindered me from Your perfect plan. There may be some things in my life I need to get rid of in order to possess all that You have for me. I cannot enter the promised land while in bondage, so I ask You now to deliver me. Lord, be merciful to me. Deliver me from the hand of my enemies. Remove far from me those who come to kill, steal, and destroy in my life (John 10:10). Just like You rescued the Israelites with a Strong Arm, I pray that You would rescue me with a Mighty Arm. Show no mercy to the demons that have tormented me and my family. Show no mercy to the enemy of my soul but with an Outstretched Arm destroy them and all their plans for my life and my family. God, pour out Your wrath upon them as You spoke in Psalm 18.

Prayer excerpt from Psalm 18 or you can read it from your Bible.

Lord, You are my Rock and my Deliverer. You are my Refuge, my Shield, and my Salvation. I call upon You now in my distress. I cry out to You. Oh Lord, I know that You hear my voice. Yes, my cry is before You. The Earth trembles and the mountains shake; they tremble because You are angry. Smoke is rising from Your Nostrils and a consuming fire comes from Your Mouth; burning coals blazed out of It. You part the Heavens and come down; dark clouds are under Your Feet. You fly now on Your heavenly creatures and soar on the wings of the wind all to come and rescue me. Fiery hailstones and lightning bolts go before You. Your anger is kindled against my enemies. Reach down from Heaven and pull me out of my troubles. Rescue me from my powerful enemies, from all who work against me. Lord, You are my Support. Lord, bring me to a place of abundance; rescue me because You delight in me. Forgive my sin and give me a clean heart before You. Make me blameless in Your Sight, for You are faithful to those who are faithful to You. Shine Your Light into any darkness in my life, for Lord, You are my Light. Your Way is perfect and there is no God besides You. It is You who arm me with strength and keep my way secure. You make my feet like the feet of a deer and cause me to leap over walls. You trained my hands for battle. Your Righthand sustains me and Your help makes me great. I pursue my enemies and overtake them. I will not turn back until they are all destroyed. I crush all my enemies now so that they cannot rise; I make them like the dust before the wind. I destroy all of them now. Lord, let us defeat them so badly that they cry out for help but there is no help for them. I trample them like mud in the streets. You have delivered me and have made me the head. The Lord lives. I give You all my praise, for You are my Rock. Be exalted oh God, for You have saved me from my enemies.

If you wish, you can open your Bible and pray Psalms 18 out loud. Do so as many times as you need.

Lord Jesus, by Your power, I ask that you break every chain off of my life right now. Destroy every spiritual yoke of bondage that has had me going in the wrong direction. Every demon, every chain, everything from darkness that has operated in my life, I rebuke you now in the mighty Name of the Lord Jesus Christ. [Repeat as many times as you feel led by God. Also, repeat and target your specific issues, such as poverty.]

Not in my power; not in my authority; not in my name; but in the Name that is above every name, the Name of the Lord Jesus Christ, I come against poverty, lack, and everything working against my financial freedom. The Lord Jesus rebukes you. Holy Spirit, I ask that you cast them out of my life right now in Jesus' Name. I pray for the Fire of God to come down and consume anything in my life that is not of God. Lord, pour out the Fire of the Holy Spirit on me now and destroy anything in my life that comes from darkness – destroy poverty, destroy anything devouring my finances, destroy delay and setback. For Your Word declares that it is not by might nor by power but by Your Spirit – so I ask that Your Spirit will drive out of me any darkness and lead me to victory in Jesus Name.

I ask you Heavenly Father to reach into my past and destroy every satanic covenant. Heavenly Father, remember me in Your abundant mercy and deliver me from my enemies.

I pray against the spirit of poverty. I break every mindset of poverty right now in Jesus Name. Father, I ask that I would be dedicated to Your Word that it would fill my life and undo the mindset of poverty. Even now, I pray that You will remove every seed the enemy has planted in my mind that has given me the wrong mindset. Free me from every stronghold of poverty in the Name Jesus Christ my Lord.

I ask You now Lord, to send your angels to deliver me. I pray that Your angels would watch over me day and night and that they will wage war against my enemies. Every day, I ask that You send Your angels to help me and fight for me.

Lord Jesus, give me visions and dreams from you. Stir up my heart with the love for Your Word and Your ways. Give me divine ideas that will propel me forward in life. Send the right people and opportunities my way and block every person or opportunity that the devil wants to send.

Thank You for making me new and for delivering me. Now Lord I ask that you lead me to the right ministry, church, or people that will help me continue my walk of freedom, in Jesus' Name I pray. AMEN (Amen means let what I have said happen.)

Repeat this prayer as often as you want – pray it daily. It does not have to be word for word; it is more important to pray following the leading of the Holy Spirit.

Side note – some say that you should not repeat a prayer because it shows a lack of faith. While this sometimes can be true, it is not always the case with repeated prayers. When the Bible says in Matthew 7:7a, "Ask and it will be given to you", the word "ask" means to keep on asking or to ask continually. It also means to crave. So, ask and keep on asking; crave your freedom and your next level in God. Seek it out, and you will get it. He is too Faithful to let you down. He is too Merciful to ignore you. You will get your desires from God if you follow Him. He loves you too much to leave you where you are. Keep praying diligently day and night.

Your Freedom

The devil knows that Jesus Christ died and rose from the dead to set the captives free. You are free. Let it be to you according to your faith (Matthew 9:29). So many Christians are bound by poverty. It is your time to be free. Walk in freedom. Remind yourself multiple times a day that Jesus has made you free. Repeat Scriptures of freedom to yourself throughout the day. The enemy is constantly plotting against us so we must be intentional to keep our freedom and possess our destinies. Fight for what you desire.

Fight God's way. Below are the basic, foundational principles to a life of freedom.

1. **Pray each day.** Pray without ceasing. Enjoy spending time with God with no distractions. This is your one-on-one time with your Father. It is your date with Him and your appointment, so you want to keep it.

2. **Pray in your heart throughout the day.** Talk to God as you go about your normal daily and nightly routines. Speak with Him about everything going on with you. Share your thoughts, desires, feelings... everything. Consider Him your new best friend that goes everywhere with you.

3. **Study your Bible daily.** Many Christians say they do not hear the voice of God. If this is you, it could be a sign that you need to spend more time in His Word. Your time in His written Word is directly connected to your ability to hear His Voice. As you grow deeper in the Word, you grow closer to God. Do not read your Bible out of obligation. Instead, study the Word, plant it in your heart and believe what it says. Notice that my instruction to you is to study your Bible, not just read it. The Bible does not instruct us to read but to study. There is a difference. You read the paper, an article, or a blog. But you study for a

test. Study the Word of God so that you learn it and know it. Store it in your heart. Desire to change so that your life aligns more and more with the Word. This is how we grow.

4. **Meditate on God's Word throughout the day.** That is, repeat the Scriptures to yourself throughout the day. You should do this out loud as often as you can but if at times you are in public, meditate on His Word in your heart. In fact, God instructed Joshua that to find good success and prosperity, he should meditate on the Word day and night. God made it clear – His method to success and prosperity revolves around His Word. Therefore, spend time in His Word, speaking It to yourself daily.

5. **When the enemy attacks, confess the Word of God.** When you are tempted, confess the Word of God. When an old mindset tries to return, confess the Word of God. Never stop confessing the Word out loud and in your heart. The Word is a powerful weapon. Use it to fight when the enemy comes against you. When you feel discouraged, use the Word to fight. God is for you. You will see your dreams come true. You will leave out your days in peace and abundance. God will respond to His Word, so speak it daily.

Do not forget to head over to the Workbook to complete the questions and exercises for this chapter. We will go deeper into your personal freedom. Very exciting and powerful!

CHAPTER 5

Restoration

"So I will restore to you the years that the swarming locust has eaten, the crawling locust, the consuming locust, and the chewing locust, My great army which I sent among you. You shall eat in plenty and be satisfied, and praise the Name of the Lord your God, Who has dealt wondrously with you; and My people shall never be put to shame."
Joel 2:25-26 (NKJV)

Do you have regrets? Have you ever wondered what life would have been like had you done things differently? Well, you are not alone. Most people have a list of regrets in their life. If you are like me, then you had many dreams for your future when you were a child. I dreamt of the house I would live in, the lifestyle I would have, the ministry I would build, and even the businesses I would own. I even dreamt of my wedding day and the gown I would wear.

Yes, I am a dreamer. I dream of aspirations and achievements to accomplish at different age milestones. But oftentimes, big dreams can bring even bigger disappointments and we give birth to this nagging voice called regret. Regret is that monster that constantly reminds you of what you could have had or should have had. Regret is a form of torment because who can go back and change the past? It is torturous to live a life of regret and today, you will be delivered from regret's sting.

As we open the Scriptures to the book of the prophet Joel, we see a despondent picture painted for us. The country and the people were in despair. Poverty was everywhere and the anointing was drained. The people and nation were not only suffering financially, but they were in a spiritual drought. The "churches", so to speak, were getting emptier by the day. There was no growth nor was anyone flourishing or advancing. The trees were withered and even the animals were starving. Not only were the people poor, but so were the animals. The land was in a state of ruins and devastation that not even an offering was available in the House of The Lord. In those days, because the people highly honored God, giving an offering was the first act of spending anyone did after they were "paid". The fact that the Scripture says there was no offering implies that they had nothing. In other words, their jobs could not afford to pay them a salary, their bank accounts were depleted, and they had no means to pay any bills or even provide food for themselves and their loved ones. They were broke!

Amid the despair, God saw and He responded to them. The One and Only real Superhero stepped in to save the day, just like He will do for you. God revealed a wonderful plan to rescue them and to bless them with more than they could imagine. Before giving them this weighty promise, He first made a request of them. What is that request? He asked that they call a fast and consecrate themselves.

"Even now," declares the LORD, "return to Me with all your heart, with fasting and weeping and mourning." Rend your heart and not your garments. Return to the LORD your God, for He is gracious and compassionate, slow to anger and abounding in love, and He relents from sending calamity. Who knows? He may turn and relent and leave behind a blessing— grain offerings and drink offerings for the LORD your God.
Joel 2:12-14 (NIV)

In Joel 2, God is asking the people to repent and turn back to Him wholeheartedly.

So many things have pulled us away from the things of God. So many distractions in our daily lives hinder us from going forward and being all He has called us to be. It is a crucial step when you decide to return to God with <u>ALL</u> your heart, giving Him every part of it. We as believers need to realize that He is our God and that He is more important than our social lives, our jobs, our cell phones, our social media accounts, the television and our favorite TV shows, video games, our friends, our reputation, our education, our titles, etc. It is a pivotal point when we realize that He comes before everything else in our lives. We make time for everything important to us and when we return to the Lord with our hearts, we then make time for Him daily above everything else. He becomes our number one priority and rightfully so.

God is waiting for us to realize He is not just some option we have; He is not a mystical mystery from the past we follow out of tradition. He wants His people to realize He is God Almighty, the Maker of Heaven and Earth and everything in between and all around. He holds the stars in His Hands and possesses the ability to do any and everything we desire. He is that God Who promised to grant us all the desires of our hearts with no limits or hesitation (Psalm 37:4). He is the One willing to take down anything that stands in the way of your blessing, eager to bless you, advance you, and prosper you at any cost. But there is a stipulation – will you return to Him with all your heart? Will you love Him more than everything else? Will you love Him more than money, fame, your reputation, your cell phone, your favorite TV shows, your favorite celebrities, even your own self? Will you put Him above all else?

"Rend your hearts and not your garments," He cries out. For the Lord is seeking those whose hearts are for Him, not just those who go through the motions. There are many people who can pretend to love God and act spiritually, but God is saying enough with the fakeness. He is concerned with our hearts because our hearts hold what we love and the essence of who we are. He has this keen ability to search the hearts of mankind and find the hidden things that lie within. He sees your motives and the intentions of your heart. He sees it all, yet He says, "return to Me."

So, will you? Will you return to the Lord? Decide now that you will put Him first. That you will seek Him above all else. You may feel the need to fast and fasting is such a beautiful thing. When coupled with prayer and the Word, there is no greater tool we can use to accomplish impossible and mighty things on earth.

Fasting, prayer, and the Word are my tag team trio for supernatural breakthroughs and to experience the impossible.

If you feel stuck, if you feel as though you have not progressed despite your desire and efforts, then *honey*, you might be in need of a fast. Fasting causes yokes and bondage to be shattered off our lives. Fasting, when done correctly, builds up our faith, weakens the carnal nature, and strengthens our spirit being. Consecrate yourself to God. Repent now for not always putting Him first and ask Him to help you daily to serve Him righteously.

Here are some points below to help you "rend your heart" before God daily:

- Dedicate a set time of day, each day to pray. Do the same for studying your Bible. You should pray and study the Word of God daily. There is no other way to grow in Him. There is no option to compromise or even miss a day. See this as important as eating and breathing. Your spiritual life depends on it even more than your body depends on food and oxygen.

- Remove from your life things that are contrary to God and your faith. You may be aware of some of these contrary things. The hidden sins, the mistakes you repeatedly make, the excuses you make to remain at a level that you expired from a long time ago. It is time to grow and move up, but you need to make those changes. Sometimes it may hurt and that is okay. After pain comes growth if you remain faithful to Jesus Christ.

- This one is tough but some of you have people in your lives that you need to separate from (and no, I am not talking about your spouse… nice try.) But on a serious note, there are friends you hang onto that are holding you back. Some even lead you into sin. Growing comes with pain and we all must experience this – parting from those who were not designed to go with us to the next level. Some people were good at your previous level, but to go up higher, you cannot take them with you. Pray for them and continue to love them because love is of God, but you have to part from them to receive that next-level blessing. Take a look at Abraham and Lot. They prospered tremendously but reached a level where they could no longer remain in the same place together. Although Abraham did not want to, He had to split from Lot. If he remained with Lot, then he would not have had the capacity to carry the blessings God had in store for him. **I repeat, if Abraham remained with Lot, there would have been no room for God to continue to prosper him.** The Bible says the land could not carry both of them. Land can represent the heart. In this context, Abraham had to separate from Lot so his heart was able to receive more from God. Lot represents his past life as well as his flesh and carnal nature. As long as he was with Lot, he plateaued. He was at his ceiling and could not go much further. Lot was comfortable for a season and God allowed it. **But there comes a point when God is ready to release so much on you that He needs your whole heart to turn back to Him.** The "Lots" in your life occupying space in your heart must move out. The things you are putting before God must receive their eviction notice and get out of the way. Why? So you can get ready and be prepared for your outpour and overflow.

Do you feel led by God to fast? Go for it! Do not talk yourself out of it, like we typically do. I would recommend reading a book on fasting such as *"Your God is Your Belly"* written by my dad, **R. Frederick Capitolin.** I can tell you that the author spends more days in the year fasting than he does eating so he knows a thing or two about fasting. He is an expert faster.

Here are a few success tips on fasting:

- To fast is to abstain from food and carnal pleasure. Many people speak of fasting certain types of foods while eating others. Personally, I do not agree with this. For example, many Christians will say they are fasting meat but eating everything else. This is not a fast. If you are still enjoying food, you are not fasting because the flesh is still being satisfied. You must be hungry on a fast; you must experience wanting food and be denied. This is what makes it a sacrifice and this is what Heaven responds to.

Fast within your ability of course (start where you can), but do not be afraid to push yourself.

- Fasting is only effective when coupled with praying and studying the Word – every day. Otherwise, you are just starving yourself. The power behind fasting is to weaken the flesh while strengthening the spirit. Starving your flesh weakens it and prayer with the Word strengthens your spirit. Spend more time praying and studying the Word so you are growing spiritually. When you do this, fasting expedites your spiritual growth.

- You must shut off secular distractions such as TV, non-Christian music, hanging out with friends, social media (except when using for work and ministry only), video games, etc. The idea is to "kill" the flesh and empower the spirit. If you are still feeding the flesh, then it slows down the effectiveness of your fast and in some cases, it hinders your fast completely. For example, if you are fasting but still watching TV, it will erase any benefits you received from the fast.

- Use the time you would spend eating, preparing meals, and performing secular activities to spend more time praying and studying the Word. So instead of getting on the couch and watching your favorite show, play some worship music and worship God around your house; or get on the couch with your Bible and notebook and study the Scriptures, making sure you are actually learning and not just reading out of obligation. If you have questions as you study, write them down, ask the Holy Spirit, and trust God to provide an answer in His time.

We have thoroughly discussed consecration and fasting and I am sure you are waiting for what's next. As we continue to walk through Joel, the request to fast and consecrate does not come empty-handed. I have outlined below the promises God made to His people through the prophet Joel as a result of them returning to Him with all their hearts. We will explore what they mean for your life and future.

Promises of God to Restore

1. Satisfied with grain, new wine, and oil.
2. Remove your shame.
3. Remove far from you all your enemies.
4. Eliminate fear.
5. Bring you joy and gladness.
6. The trees will bear their fruit and yield their strength; the pastures will spring up.
7. Provide both the former rain and the latter rain.
8. The threshing floors will be full of wheat.

9. Your storage barrels will overflow with new wine and oil.
10. The years the locusts ate will be restored.
11. You will eat in plenty and be satisfied.
12. You will praise the Name of The Lord.
13. You will know that God is in the midst of you.
14. You will know that there is no one like Him.
15. You will never be ashamed again.

We will explore each of these in more detail shortly, and what they mean for you.

Everything they lost or that they should have had, God promised to restore it to them. But this was not a one-for-one restoration – He promised an overflow. An exceedingly abundantly above all they could ask or think type of restoration (Ephesians 3:20, NKJV). If they lost one million God replaced it with ten million, for example.

There is a critical point on restoration I want you to understand. The word restore means to bring back; to return to a former condition; to put someone back in possession of something (Merriam-Webster Dictionary[4]). You might be thinking, "Well, I never had it so how is God restoring it?" Recall earlier in this book we discussed how God knew you before you were in your mother's womb? When the Almighty God placed you on this Earth, He placed your destiny inside of you. This is why the Scripture can say,

> *"Remember the former things of old:*
> *for I am God, and there is none else;*
> *I am God, and there is none like me,*
> *Declaring the end from the beginning,*
> *and from ancient times the things that are not yet done,*
> *saying, My counsel shall stand,*
> *and I will do all my pleasure."*
> *Isaiah 46:9-10 (NKJV)*

God declared your end at your beginning. Before you were in your mother's womb, He knew you; He declared your destiny, He declared your purpose, He gave you your calling and your gifts. He declared your spouse and the blessings over your children and your generations; He declared the life you would live, the souls you would touch, the companies you would work for and the companies you would own; He declared the houses you would have and the houses you would give away to the needy; He declared the justice you would fight for and the change you would bring; He declared every day of your life from the moment you were born to the moment He would call your spirit back to Him.

Here is where the problem comes in. The devil and his demons are spirits and see as spirits. They, therefore, can see what God has placed in you, even when you cannot see it, and they attack the destiny that is resting on you. This is why fear comes – it sees your God-given ability and future and wants to do everything it can to stop you. So it creates lies and a false reality but makes it feel real to you. Demons appeal to your emotions because most humans are undisciplined in their emotions – we act on how we feel versus acting on faith in God and wisdom. This is how the devil steals from us. He tricks us with lies to stop us. When we stop, that is, we do not move forward to fulfill our dreams and callings, he has just robbed us of it.

This is also where some trials and challenges come in. The devil sets situations up in our lives to discourage us and to cause us to change our focus. He creates problems as distractions so that we focus on the situation and not on our destiny. He tries to make us focus on current things – what we can see and feel – to hinder us from the pursuit of our destiny and without even realizing it, we neglect our destiny. But if we will trust in God no matter what comes our way and keep our eyes on our Lord Jesus and the Word He has spoken concerning us, we will not fall for the enemy's traps.

When our God promises to restore us, He is not only referring to what you had and lost in the natural realm. He is including everything He gave to you in the spirit realm that did not become a reality in the natural.

What have you lost that you need to be restored? What are your dreams in life that you have not yet attained? At this place in your life, you might have hoped that you were further along and that you had more wealth, more success, a family, a thriving ministry, etc. What has the devil stolen from you? What are the blessings that God laid out for you to receive that the devil tricked you out of through fear, deception, lies, and stagnation? There are dreams inside you and desires you daydream about, some of which you might have even given up on. You might have stopped daydreaming, but I want you to muster all the strength inside of you and hear the voice of God for you today. Your God will restore!

Dream again of your greatest desires and wishes. Dig back into your childhood before you were told you could not; before you were given a limitation; before life's situations tried to destroy you. Uncover your inner dreams. They reveal your purpose. They are like flashlights directing you to the things God placed in you to bring to the world. You cannot leave this world with them inside of you. Your enemy who has tried to stop you is worthy of nothing but your laughter – so go ahead and laugh in his face. (Seriously, go ahead and laugh in his face… We'll wait). What he tried to keep from you and what he stole from you, God will restore all to you, and even more. So. Much. More.

> *"Now to Him who is able to do exceedingly abundantly above all that we ask or think, according to the power that works in us, to Him be glory in the church by Christ Jesus to all generations, forever and ever. Amen."*
>
> *Ephesians 3:20 – 21 (NKJV)*

When God restores you, He will get all the glory. It will be obvious that the blessings flowing into your life are not by natural means but supernatural. They will be so extraordinary and over the top, that all will know that it is the Hand of God on your life, and in this way, His Name will be glorified.

Let us explore each restoration promise from the Prophet Joel below.

#1 Satisfied with Grain, New Wine, and Oil

The first promise God made in the Joel prophecy is to restore the grain, the new wine, and the oil. As an agricultural society, the people grew grain, vineyards from which they produced wine, and olive trees from which they made oil. All of these were destroyed by the locusts. To give them back the grain, new wine, and oil, is to give them their lives back. God promises to give you back your career, your business, your family, your activities, and everything that makes you, you. God wants to restore you to the place you <u>should</u> have been had the enemy not stopped you, had you not been delayed, had you not been afraid, and had you not been robbed. When He restores the grain, the wine, and the oil, just like everything else, He places you where you should be. He eliminates all the mistakes you made and all the delays you suffered and expedites you to your rightful place spiritually, martially, financially, professionally, educationally, and in every area of your life. He gives you the house you should have owned five years ago, the cars that should have already been in your possession, the title you should be identified by, the income you should have, the business you were supposed to have had ten years ago, the spouse you prayed for, the children your body longed to produce, the ministry you were called to do, and everything else.

We saw earlier in the text that the grain, wine, and oil were offerings that the people brought to the priests. The Bible describes their destitute state as them not having an offering to bring to the House of The Lord. In reality, the first thing God was restoring was His offering. By filling their barns with wheat, which can be referred to in modern times as filling their bank accounts with money, He gives them provisions so that they have money to bring to the House of God. As He gives to you, give back to Him.

God wants His house wealthy and to accomplish this, He makes the people who frequent it wealthy so they can bring an offering.

The more you have, the more you are expected to give. So, the more He gives you, the more He can expect from you. He honors His offering and those who respect the offering of God are blessed to prosper. Those who dishonor His offering, who put no thought to it, are dishonored by God. Here is what God spoke regarding Eli the priest's sons. They were known for disobeying God's commandments regarding the offering.

> *"Why do you scorn [hate] my sacrifice and offering that I prescribed for my dwelling?... Those who honor me I will honor, but those who despise me will be disdained [despised, lowly esteemed]."*
> 1 Samuel 2:29, 30b (NKJV)

So, as you come into blessings, do not forget to honor God with your increase by giving to Him the portion due unto Him with respect.

The grain is so important. It represents you and your everyday life. Also, in the New Testament Jesus spoke of grain as people. We see here in Matthew 3:12 how Jesus Christ describes wheat (grain) in one of His famous teachings:

> *"His winnowing fan is in His hand, and He will thoroughly clean out His threshing floor, and gather His wheat into the barn; but He will burn up the chaff with unquenchable fire."* (NKJV)

He teaches on separating the wheat from the chaff. Here we see the wheat represents you and me, those who believe in Him and are saved. The chaff represents the people who are not saved. The restoration of the wheat means God wants to make you whole again. He will heal the broken places of your life and mend you together into the wonderful work of art you are meant to be. The right people will flow into your life, ministry, and business. You, your ministry, your family, and your business will flourish.

Wine is often referred to in the Scripture as joy. Here, while God is referring to the literal wine, we can also see the symbolism in this. Could you use some extra wine in your life? I do not mean the drink. When Jesus pours out wine on you, He is filling your spirit with gladness and laughter. You will have nothing to cry about. His joy will overflow in you and no one will be able to stop your gladness. This joy, the world does not give it to you and the world cannot take it away. Please note that I am not making a case for drinking alcohol as I do not drink alcohol myself.

Oil signifies the anointing and your spiritual walk with God. He wants to restore your prayer life, your studying of the Word, and He wants to use you in the way He intended. He wants to fulfill your destiny and the purpose for which He created you. When anyone was called to serve The Lord, from the priest to the king, they were always anointed with oil. It symbolized that God was with this person and that He would work through them while they served in their role.

By restoring your oil, God is placing His anointing on your life and making a declaration that not only is He with you always as He promised but that He will work through you and with you in all that you do. He will establish your plans and bring them to pass. He sees your dreams and desires and will anoint you to go forward and make them come true. He has paved the way for you and made your way smooth.

The vision God showed me on restoring the grain, wine, and oil is that your life is where you want it to be and more importantly, where God wants it to be. This includes material things. You are living the life you have dreamt of and your joy is complete.

#2 – Remove Your Shame

This is an easy one. God loves to erase the shame of those who follow Him. Those who looked down on you and had negative things to say about you; the teachers and professors who did not believe you could amount to anything great; the boss that fired you and mistreated you; those who sat around waiting for you to fail; they will see you rise to your rightful place in life. God will erase the negative words they spoke concerning you and their expectations of failure for your future.

One of the most famous Scriptures in the Bible is The Lord is my Shepherd – Psalm 23. In it, King David says that God prepares a table before him in the presence of his enemies. Right in the face of your enemies, God will lay out a feast of abundance for you. His provision and abundance in your life will be seen by all and it is all for His glory.

There is also a hidden shame that God wants to erase. It is something that many people carry secretly. It might be related to a hidden sin, a secret from your past, or a hardship you are currently going through. Whatever it may be, it places you in a place of shame; it causes you to feel less than others or inadequate; it may also give you something to hide and adds a few sentences to your story that you wish were not there. Even the hidden shame that no one may know about, God promises to erase from your life when He restores you.

Pray to the Lord now and ask Him to erase your shame, even the hidden ones.

"Lord Jesus, I ask You now to erase my shame. I give You the burdens I have carried. Remove far from me the shame of what other people did that hurt me, the shame of my own mistakes, and the shame of my

shortcomings, difficulties, and afflictions. Please free me that I no longer carry this burden and weight. I receive Your peace in place of that shame, guilt, and hurt. In Jesus Name! Amen."

Believe that you have received His peace and if you should experience a feeling of shame again, remind shame that Jesus has given you His very own peace in that area.

#3 and 4 – Remove Your Enemies and Fear

The same spiritual forces that hindered you, including fear, will have to face the judgment of God. He will remove them far from you and my prayer is that the vengeance of God shows no mercy to them so much that they regret ever getting in your way. I love that the Scriptures call out fear specifically.

Fear is so deceptive. It convinces you of an untruth, gets you to believe it as true, and then uses your faith in it to destroy you and steal from you.

It is probably the most widely used tool of the enemy to stop people. God says, "Start a business" then fear says, "But you're not qualified. How are you going to get the funds? You don't have the time. You can't do it." God says, "Go back to school". Fear says, "You're not smart enough. You can't afford it. You can't compete with the other students". God says, "Start a ministry" but fear rears its ugly head and convinces you that you just don't have what it takes. God wants you to step out of your comfort zone but here comes fear convincing you that you should just keep things as they are and not venture out.

Fear robs people of their destinies by stopping them from doing what God has enabled them to do through their faith in Christ Jesus. We have a whole chapter where we deal with fear and I believe that if you struggle with it, through the teachings in this book, you will be set free.

#5 – Bring Joy and Gladness

God specifically calls out joy and gladness as part of the restoration package. This needs no explaining, right? He simply wants to make you happy. Happiness does not come from doing whatever you want. True happiness comes from doing the will of God for your life. This is where you find fulfillment.

A statement that I sincerely dislike is, "Do what makes you happy." Or in speaking with a loved one concerning a decision they are facing, one responds with, "Whatever makes you happy." Living life doing whatever makes you happy is selfish and carnal and your happiness becomes circumstantial. Your temporary happiness can lead to sin, misery, and move you further out of the plan and purpose of God for your life. You must find out the will of God for your life and follow after it. Do not do whatever makes you happy. Instead, do what pleases God. Do what makes Jesus happy. Then you will find true happiness that cannot be taken away, no matter what happens in your life. Selah.

#6 - The Trees Will Bear Their Fruit and Yield Their Strength; the Pastures Will Spring up

Trees have always been a symbol of prosperity, productivity, and multiplication. They are a beautiful creation and very powerful in meaning. Every tree starts as a seed. The seed of a tree is planted, watered, and cared for. It then produces a tree which then produces more of the same fruit. The fruit provides food for both people and animals. Trees provide a place of lodging for other animals and rest for people in its shade. So, what does all this mean for you? This is an overflow.

To differentiate, the grain, wine, and oil we discussed earlier are for your sustenance. They are representations of the things that pertain to your everyday life. Number six here goes beyond sustaining you. It is beyond abundance in your everyday life and introduces a new level of prosperity that not only sustains you but provides abundantly for others. Your children and grandchildren will be set up with a rich inheritance; your community and those around you will flourish because of your blessings; you can support Kingdom work to a much greater and more impactful degree.

Trees are all about producing more and more (multiplication) and producing so much that it provides abundance for others. From one tree can come several forests. This is because God made it to bear fruit with its seed inside of it, as we see in Genesis chapter 1. Those seeds continue bearing more fruit that contains more seeds that can go on to bear more fruit.

This is how God wants to bless you, where your blessing produces more blessings that spread out from you and reach the lives of others. You can provide scholarships to children to send them to school; you can pay off the debts of others; you can provide for a poor family who needs help; you can buy a car for a person who desperately needs it; you can rebuild the school in your neighborhood that is falling apart; provide for missionaries in foreign countries; pay the rent of the person who sits next to you in church who does not know how they are going to make ends meet; buy houses for those in need; and so much more. You will be able to fund the work of the Kingdom and advance God's purposes and will on the Earth.

#7 – The Former and Latter Rains

While rain is a vital component of the life of any seed, here God does not just promise rain. He promises both the former and the latter rains. The former rain came first and supplied water so that the crops produced a harvest. The latter rain was considered a luxury. If it came, it meant the crops would be more abundant. They would be bigger, plumper, juicer, and in greater quantity than they would have been with just the former rain. I hope by now you are seeing the theme of ABUNDANCE! God does not want to simply bless you; He wants you to have more than enough in great quantities. God is the "Go Big or Go Home" kind of God. He wants every area of your life to be fruitful, to multiply, and to bring abundance. But here is my favorite part of this promise. God said He will send both types of rains *in the same month*. WOW! That, my friend, is an *expedited blessing*. Not only is He promising abundance, but God is saying I want it to come quickly. Selah and Shout!

Can I prophesy for a minute? You have been delayed for too long. You have been waiting for too long. You have been at the back of the line for too long. This is your time. I am not being cliché. This is a promise of God written in Scripture for you and if you will choose to believe and put your faith in our Lord Jesus Christ and His Word, I declare over your life right now the abundance that He promises. I speak over you good success, joy, gladness, peace, wealth, prosperity, good health, a healthy marriage, Godly children, and every "good and perfect" thing (James 1:17). And I speak it into your life NOW! Not a year from now, but NOW! In this time and in this season of your life. I declare it now in Jesus' Name! Amen.

#8 and 9 - The Threshing Floor and Storage Barrels will Overflow

Numbers 8 and 9 reiterate what we stated in number 1 – that God will provide wheat, which is also grain, new wine, and oil. I love that He reiterates it here. Whenever God says anything, it is so. When He says something twice it confirms with no doubt that it is established and cannot be changed and that He will do it quickly. Here is what Joseph said about Pharaoh's dream – God gave Him the same message in two dreams.

"And the dream was repeated to Pharaoh twice because the thing is established by God, and God will shortly bring it to pass."
Genesis 42:32 (NKJV)

God repeated the promises to them because it is set in stone and no one can stop it – not even the devil in all his schemes – and God plans to do it now.

#10 - The Years the Locusts ate Will be Restored

This is where regrets must leave you in Jesus' Name. God's heart for you is so enormous. He wants to bless you in more ways than you can imagine. God is not hung up on your mistakes because He sees the whole picture. He sees how your story ends so He is not moved by your past. The years that you lost, the time you think you wasted, the time you spent suffering, the time spent in hardship, none of it was wasted. God says He will restore it all to you.

Sometimes we think, "where would I be today had I…" But today I challenge you to stop thinking this way. This is an attack of the enemy on your mind to keep you bound. Do you think your mistakes are big enough to stop the Almighty God? Well, they are not. His plan for you still stands. He has not changed His mind about you. He loves you dearly and wants to see great things happen for you. He is right there with you and He will give back to you all the time you think you wasted or lost. There is nothing to regret when your God says that He will give it all back to you, miraculously restore all the years you lost, and place you right where you would have been had everything worked out perfectly in the first place and had you not made those mistakes. I love this part of the story. This is so amazing to me. This is how much He loves you. It blows my mind that God does this for us but I have seen Him do it so many times and you are no exception.

Someone that I know dropped out of college and took years to finally get back in school and graduate. He felt delayed and behind as he was in school with a younger generation and then graduating to compete for jobs with them. This man was a believer in Christ and prayed for God's restoration. Here is how God answered. Upon graduation, he was given a role as a manager and it came with a manager's salary. Though he was delayed, God placed him right where he would have been had he graduated at age 22 with his friends. Even his finances were restored because God blessed him with a salary that most people have to work several years post-graduation to obtain. God is tremendously good and He will do the same for you, even more, if you have the faith. And how do you get the faith? By reading, studying, and meditating on the Word of God, choosing to believe it above the lies the enemy has told you; by reading books like this that boost your faith; by obeying the written and spoken Word of God; and through prayer and thanksgiving.

He will put you in the place where you were supposed to be all along. It will be as though you were never delayed. The years and everything else the locust ate, will be given back to you! The locust destroyed crops that took many years to grow. They destroyed gardens and fields that the people thought could not be restored. But God is so miraculous! He restored the land and all they had and so much more. Isaiah 61:7, paraphrased, says God gives you double for your trouble. This means that you had to suffer a little longer because your blessings were delayed and you went through some things that you should not have gone through. As a result of that, God in His abundant goodness decided to double your blessings just to make up for what you went through. So in reality, you actually end up better off in the end. With that awesome revelation, there is absolutely nothing to regret but to rejoice that

God is going to bless you even more because although you were delayed, you have returned to Him with your whole heart.

As we saw earlier, He promised the latter and former rains in the same month, which is an expedited blessing. There may be things in your life that you think are past repairing. Things the enemy destroyed that are like the fields of the Israelites – it took years to build and now that it is destroyed it seems impossible to repair. With God, nothing is impossible. God will work on your behalf and restore even the things that we think are past repair. God will rebuild the fields of your life. Put your faith in Him and nothing will be impossible. Even now, He is repairing and mending in your life. Trust Him and He will bring it to pass.

#11. You Will Eat in Plenty and be Satisfied

You will be full and satisfied. God wants to not only take care of your daily needs but bring fullness and satisfaction to you. To be full means you lack nothing. It is what King David spoke of at the beginning of the twenty-third Psalm,

"The Lord is my Shepherd, I shall not want." (KJV)

"The Lord is my best friend and Shepherd. I always have more than enough." (TPT)

I quoted this text here in two translations because many people are familiar with the first translation, the King James, but most do not understand what it means. The phrase "I shall not want" means I will have everything I could ever possibly need and therefore I lack nothing. **When God is through restoring you, there is nothing left for you to want and desire.** You will be full. God's plan for your life is always bigger than you think. If you will trust and follow Him, He will fulfill His plans in you and you will reach a state of complete satisfaction.

#12 You Will Praise the Name of the Lord Your God

Why does God do all that He does for you? Why does He advance, prosper, and bring you into the fullness of who He is? It is to bring glory to His Name. The world has to know who Jesus is. They need to know our God Yahweh and they see Him in us. Your success brings Him Glory. First, when God performs all that it is He desires to do for you, you will be unrecognizable. I love seeing the lives of people God has transformed. You know without any doubt that this change, this new level, must have occurred by supernatural means. God does much more than you or I can do in our lives so that when we see it and when others witness it, they know that it had to have been God.

There is a woman named Ananya. She came from a poor family and failed in school. She was often told that she was not intelligent and will never have a bright future. Ananya struggled for years with self-worth issues, anger, and hurt. BUT GOD! She gave her life to Jesus and decided to trust Him. This same woman who dropped out of school and was told she would never succeed at anything started her own business and is now a millionaire. It took a short time for her to make her first one million dollars. The same ones who put her down and mocked her have never seen anything close to a million dollars. **When God gets in your situation and you decide to trust Him, the sky is not even a limit – there is no limit.** She knows only because of Jesus she is successful, so she gives Him all the glory.

#13 Know that God is in the Midst of You

The Israelites went through seasons with God. At times, His Presence was strong amongst them and He moved throughout the land by means of anointed vessels – His prophets and judges. When God was with them, they never lost a battle. They were prospering. Everything they did succeeded and every enemy that came against them lost. Even the neighboring nations knew when the Lord was with Israel – Israel prospered above the other nations and was supernaturally protected. Their covering from God defied science and logic. Famine could be prevalent in all the lands, but it would never touch the land of the Israelites.

They had divine protection, divine provision, and divine positioning.

When God restores you, you will know Him and that He is with you always. You will not just quote the Scripture because everyone else says it, but you will have a revelation of what it truly means to have the God of the universe, the maker of Heaven and Earth stand with you in every moment of every day and every night. The God who parted the Red Sea and completely annihilated all the enemies of His people; the same God who blessed Isaac with wealth while the nation was suffering an economic crisis; that same God who caused Abraham, Isaac, and Jacob to prosper and attain great wealth; the God who healed every disease including the incurable, raised the dead, caused the lame to walk, the blind to see, and withered arms and legs to grow out – yes, that God is with you. Always.

When you receive a revelation of Who is with you, you will never see life the same. You begin to laugh at the mountains in your way. Goliath looks like an ant in front of you because you know that God Almighty, our Lord Jesus Christ is in you and surrounds you. That obstacle that dared to stand in your way is like dust before the feet of your God who goes before you. You take fierce vengeance on the fear that crippled you for so many years. You rise in power, victory, and confidence. Jehovah, Yahweh, Jesus Christ, the Almighty God, the Everlasting Father, the Ancient of Days, the Eternal One, the All-Powerful One, the All-Knowing All-Seeing God is with you. End. Of. Story!

When you understand this, you then ask yourself, "What can stop me?" Your faith increases and you step out and do the brave things God has been wanting you to do all along. You know that Yahweh is holding your hands so you are confident that you will not fail. You now move into the realm where failure is impossible.

#14 Know That There is no one Like Him

Not only do you have a revelation that He is with you, but that nothing on earth, in space, in the heavens, or in hell, is a match for God Almighty. As I mentioned before, not even the devil is a rival of God. The devil was created by God. There is no such thing as God versus the devil. God stands above all. Your problem is not a match for Him. Your difficulties are nothing before Him. Your fears do not have a say when He stands with you. No one is like The Lord our God. Believe it and then act like you believe it. Live life knowing that He is with you and He has no match. Hold your head up high and pursue your dreams.

#15 Never be Ashamed Again

We saw in the second promise of restoration that God wants to remove your shame. In His last promise, He says that you will never be ashamed again. What this truth is saying is that you will never again return to the place you were before. God will take you out of your current state with a mighty hand and by mighty miracles and restore every area of your life to its rightful place, and He will do it in such a powerful way that you will never return to the former place, ever again. He provides a lasting anointing that keeps you in your promised land and prevents you from going back to the land of bondage. Whether your bondage is poverty, stagnation, marital, family, career, ministry, all of the above, etc., they are no match for His mighty plan to restore. Every area of your life will operate as He intended it to, including your finances, and your future is free from all the struggles you faced in the past.

Please head over to the Workbook to complete your personal exercises for this chapter.

CHAPTER 6

A Healthy Relationship with Money

*"For the kingdom of heaven is like a man traveling to a far country, who called his own servants and delivered his goods to them. *[15]* And to one he gave five talents, to another two, and to another one, to each according to his own ability; and immediately he went on a journey. *[16]* Then he who had received the five talents went and traded with them, and made another five talents. *[17]* And likewise he who had received two gained two more also. *[18]* But he who had received one went and dug in the ground, and hid his lord's money. *[19]* After a long time the lord of those servants came and settled accounts with them. *[20]* So he who had received five talents came and brought five other talents, saying, 'Lord, you delivered to me five talents; look, I have gained five more talents besides them.' *[21]* His lord said to him, 'Well done, good and faithful servant; you were faithful over a few things, I will make you ruler over many things. Enter into the joy of your lord.' *[22]* He also who had received two talents*

came and said, 'Lord, you delivered to me two talents; look, I have gained two more talents besides them.' [23] *His lord said to him, 'Well done, good and faithful servant; you have been faithful over a few things, I will make you ruler over many things. Enter into the joy of your lord.'* [24] *Then he who had received the one talent came and said, 'Lord, I knew you to be a hard man, reaping where you have not sown, and gathering where you have not scattered seed.* [25] *And I was afraid, and went and hid your talent in the ground. Look, there you have what is yours.'* [26] *But his lord answered and said to him, 'You wicked and lazy servant, you knew that I reap where I have not sown, and gather where I have not scattered seed.* [27] *So you ought to have deposited my money with the bankers, and at my coming I would have received back my own with interest.* [28] *So take the talent from him, and give it to him who has ten talents.* [29] *'For to everyone who has, more will be given, and he will have abundance; but from him who does not have, even what he has will be taken away.'" Matthew 25:15-29 (NKJV)*

How do we build strong ministries? How do we take care of the poor, the orphans, and widows, and send missionaries to remote areas of the world to spread the Gospel? How do we build Godly schools to send our children to, so they are surrounded by the right values? How do we build thriving businesses, organizations, and institutions? How do we do anything great and impactful in our world? There are many answers to these questions but among them includes money. Children of God, we need money in large quantities to do what God wants us to do. It saddens me when I see the lack of spiritual, financial, and influential progress the Church has made over the decades. There was a point in time where the Church of Jesus Christ was thriving and leading in society to the point where leaders in the world came to the people of God for advice before making decisions. The Church influenced every area of society, but today it feels as though we are struggling to stay afloat at times.

There are areas in the world where there is a Church on every block but there are no Christian schools around to provide our children with the spiritual protection they need from the ungodly doctrines that public and secular schools are teaching them. The truth of the matter is that we need money to accomplish things and to influence society. I pray for my country, our leadership, and the laws that are passed. I have mentioned this before, but I wish so desperately that we had more believers who were wealthy enough to support the right political candidates and push laws that promote the Kingdom of God. The reality is many laws that are passed come from people who have the money to form the right relationship with politicians and push their motives forward.

Due to the lack of wealth and giving in the Kingdom, our progress has been stunted.

And I hear my spiritual people saying that it is a lack of praying, knowledge of the Word, and holiness that has stunted the growth in the church. I do not disagree with this, but it is obvious as well that Christianity has not advanced as much as it could have due to a lack of funds.

For example, I wish we had more financial resources to rule in entertainment and the media. Could you imagine if most TV networks, producers, and the most popular magazines were Christ-centered? Our world would be so different because the primary core of influence is Godly. Instead of lust, sexual immorality, rebellion, greed, murder, violence, divorce, and the like being spread like wildfire, we would learn principles of purity, prayer, obedience, and submission to God, love, giving, faith, marriages standing the tests of time, and other Biblical topics through the media and this would be widespread (not just a movie here and there but the primary themes in all TV). Instead, the devil has taken what was meant for us and his influence is ruling in entertainment and his doctrines have been pushed through the media for decades, to the point where it has had the biggest influence on our culture. Today, society and our culture are filled with sinful practices that are not only accepted as correct but are promoted and pushed onto people because they are made to look acceptable in the media and are presented as being right. I feel passionate about this as you can tell from me belaboring this point.

The Body of Christ needs more wealth and resources and we need to rise to places of leadership and influence. We were meant to rule across various industries so that God's rule is established on Earth in each industry and sector. It is through us that God works on the Earth and He has made everything available to us. The problem is that we have not embraced all the promises of God and stepped out in faith to do and be what He ordained for us. We do not know who we are in God and that ignorance has prevented many from walking through doors that were opened thousands of years ago on the cross.

The issue is threefold:

Issue 1: The Lack of Truth

There is a lack of truth. We have been taught false doctrines for so long that for some, it is at the root of their stagnation. The truth is that you will not get rich due to a "bank error in your favor" (Monopoly board game[5]).

If you want riches, you need a way to have a consistent inflow of wealth in your life.

You need a plan. You will not just wake up one day and discover you are a millionaire. You have to work to build that kind of wealth, knowing that God is on your side and that he has already made the way for you to prosper. He has already blessed you and your help is already waiting for you.

Issue 2: The Lack of Faith

There is a lack of faith. Faith is the currency of Heaven. If you want a miracle, you need the amount of faith that this miracle requires. I cannot walk into Louis Vuitton wanting to pay a Target price tag. I will walk out empty-handed, and this is the case with some Christians. Increase your faith through prayer and studying the Word so that you can get the things you pray for.

> *"So faith comes from hearing [what is told], and what is heard comes by the [preaching of the] message concerning Christ."*
> *Romans 10:17 (AMP)*

Jesus always said, *"He who has an ear let him hear"* (Matthew 11:15, NKJV). You need to first have ears to hear. Your heart cannot be hardened, nor can it be stubborn, otherwise, when He speaks, you will not hear. Romans 10 quoted above is essentially saying, read the Word of God and receive what it teaches, even if it means you are wrong or you have to make changes to your thinking and life. Then, you will develop ears that can hear. As you continue listening to the Word, your hearing increases and so does your faith. Bottomline – get God's Word in you and submit to it.

Issue 3: The Lack of Works

There is a lack of works, that is, doing the things we need to do in order to have what we are believing in God for. The Bible does teach that *"faith without works is dead" (James 2:17, NKJV)*. As I mentioned before, riches will not fall from the sky and land in our laps. We have to do our parts, but God will guide us along the way.

Money is meant to advance the work of God on earth and improve our way of living. It is not a want. It is a necessity. You do not just want to be rich. **You need to be rich.** You need to have an abundance. There are ministries that you need to support. There are many people waiting on you. You need to be rich so you can do God's work on Earth.

Abraham, the father of faith, died a wealthy man. He left wealth and riches for his children that passed on for many generations. I do not know about you, but I am ready to see the Church rid of generational curses and instead produce generational blessings!

"Now Abraham was <u>very rich</u> in cattle, in silver, and in gold."
Genesis 13:2 (NKJV)

Let this sink into your heart and increase your faith in God. His son Isaac prospered even more than him.

*"The man [Isaac] began to prosper, and continued prospering until he became **very prosperous**; for he had possessions of flocks and possessions of herds and a great number of servants. So the Philistines envied him."*
Genesis 26:13-14 (NKJV)

Genesis 26 says the Philistines envied Isaac and that leads me to inject this point here – one of the meanings of the word "blessed" in the Bible is to be envied. That is when God speaks of blessing you, He is speaking of giving to you what others wish they could have. The blessings of God will leave you in a place where others will wish that they could be you. I am not saying that God supports envy because envy is a sin that stems from the condition of the human heart. But this level of blessing lets the unbelieving see what your God can do and gives Him glory. It acts as a witness. It was true in the days of the Israelites after they left Egypt. The nations around them spoke highly of them and their God because they saw how greatly God prospered them. God's witness in the Earth was their deliverance and prosperity.

Here is an example to help you see this point. During the economic crisis that started in 2008 and continued for a few more years, many people lost their jobs. I recall being new in my accounting career. Many college graduates could not find jobs simply because of the economy. Not only was I employed and paid a healthy salary, I received a bonus, a promotion, and not one, but two raises. Many of my college friends wished they were in my shoes as some of them faced layoffs, could not find employment, or had frozen salaries. This is all due to the prosperity of God upon me and nothing I did. This does not have to be financial only. God's blessing spans all areas of our lives.

Take for example Samantha, who is caring for an ill husband, works full time, and has a young daughter to care for. Samantha just enrolled in a doctoral program but then suddenly learns that on top of everything she is dealing with, her husband was diagnosed with cancer. She decides to trust God and continue with her education, although the temptation was to delay her degree. In addition to all of this, Samantha is also battling a brain injury that has made it difficult at times for her to study. Well, Samantha has an average in school of 99% and is at the top of her doctorate class. How can this be? How can the woman with so much responsibility, difficulties, and so little time be number one against others who have a lot less on their plate? The grace of God! God prospered her education and no matter what the devil throws her way, the blessing of God cannot be reversed. As long as she continues to trust Him, she will always be number one. It is also worth mentioning that God touched Samantha powerfully one day and completely healed her head injury. God is still working miracles and prospering us in every area of our lives, our health included.

I wanted to add these stories to help boost your faith. But let us move on.

In the opening Scripture to this chapter, we see that the master gave three of his servants varying amounts of talents, which in the literal sense is money. This parable is about the Kingdom of God – Jesus used how the servants managed their money as a lesson for how we should manage the Kingdom of God. In the literal sense, it is about money management so we will address it in this book.

In verse 15, it says that He gave to each one *"according to His own ability."* This is important to note. God does not give us more than we can handle otherwise it would ruin us. In this parable, the master, who represents God, gave each servant only what he can handle. God will never give you millions if you can only handle hundreds. You need to properly manage the money you now have so that you are well-positioned to receive more and to properly handle the increase that God is getting ready to give you. You see that the servant who received the five talents and the one who received the two went and invested their money and it doubled in value. They were good stewards who did the right thing with the money they were given. When their master returned, he called them *"good and faithful."* Why? It was because they used wisdom to increase what God gave them.

God is all about multiplication and reproduction, not just financially but spiritually and in every area of your life. He wants to see things multiplied, which is most evident in creation. He made all of us, including plants and animals, with a purpose to produce and multiply, and then reviewed His creative work and called them good. The truth is, He does not like things to remain stagnant and stuck. Stagnation is of the devil. Lack of progress is his cousin.

This is seen in the third servant who received one talent and did nothing with it. He produced nothing more than what his master gave him. And the saddest part of the story is that he thought he was doing something good. He thought it was the right thing to do. He clearly had been taught a false doctrine and believed it. His master was upset with him and called him *"wicked and lazy."*

That seems a bit harsh, but the truth is, when we do not use what God has given to us, we are acting wickedly. We are embracing stagnation and we do not progress. We are not accomplishing God's purposes and that is exactly what the devil wants.

We are also hurting others who need our gifts, businesses, ministry, ideas, etc. God considers it wickedness for us to leave the Earth, that is to die, without using the gifts and talents that He placed inside of us and without releasing the dreams that are in our hearts.

The servant was also called lazy. He thought that because of the greatness of his master, he should just do nothing and give the master back exactly what he gave him.

How many Christians, sadly, think this way? They think that because God is All-Powerful that He will just make them whatever He wants and they have to do nothing; that if God wants them rich, He will just wave His magic wand over them and make them rich. That is a lazy mindset and this is what I refer to as "Christian laziness," where we wait on God to miraculously do for us, what we should be doing for ourselves (it certainly does not mean a person is lazy overall).

As I read that passage repeatedly, the Holy Spirit showed me something. The master gave the servants the talents and then walked away. He expected them to figure out how to use the talents and increase them. They had to learn how to invest them, whether it meant getting educated, finding a mentor, doing their research, etc. They had to put in the effort to get results. So many Christians allow Christianity to cripple them. They do nothing and expect God to do all the work. God has placed gifts, talents, ambitions, desires, businesses, skills, abilities, etc. inside of you, but He expects you to use wisdom and diligently do all the necessary work to build out these ideas. Think of an unsaved person who wants to start a business – they do all the research, put in the time and effort, and work hard to make it successful. We must do all the same work they would, *except* we pray along the way and listen to instructions from God when He gives them. We bring God into the equation every step of the way and He blesses our efforts; He aligns opportunities for us, He opens doors, He warns us of dangers and mistakes, etc. He is like a Secret Weapon to help us succeed at a greater level, but we are not exonerated of doing ALL the work.

God's help is not an excuse to be lazy. His help works on top of your efforts to bring about greater results.

I cannot emphasize this enough because too many Christians are being held back waiting on God to do for them when God is waiting on them to make a move. And not just make <u>a move</u> but make <u>all the moves</u> and do them with excellence. For example, if your talent is doing hair, you do not simply pray to own your hair salon. You also need to learn how to open a hair salon and move forward doing all the steps. Now that the salon is opened, you do not only pray, hoping God will send you clients – you must also get out there and do what is necessary to attract clients. It seems so simple but so many Christians have been deceived in this area.

Many have been waiting for wealth to show up without putting in any effort to build wealth. This must end now.

When you face God at the end of your life, what do you have to show to Him? What have you produced from the things He gave you? What have you produced from the seeds God has planted in you? The gifts, the talents, the desires, and the ideas, placed inside of you as well as the prophecies spoken concerning you– all the things He placed in your heart and mind – what account can you give? Have you been a good steward of the things He gave you? This is the time to end laziness. Stop waiting for things to just happen and be like the first two servants. They had a plan of how to use the money their master gave them. They invested it under sound wisdom and it multiplied and produced a harvest. You have to do your part with what God has given you and then you will see your harvest.

This parable can be interpreted in regard to our individual spiritual walk with God, our ministry and giftings He gave us, the skills he bestowed on us to earn income, and our overall finances. I discussed the money aspect of it because this chapter is about ruling over your finances well.

Friends, please listen to me. God has given you something. I know you prayed for millions and are waiting to see millions but let me share with you a secret of how God works. When you ask to become a millionaire, God does not give you ten million dollars. Instead, He gives you an idea or an instruction. This is a seed and that seed contains the ten million dollars. He gave the first servant five talents. The servant had to then go forward and do certain things to multiply what the master gave him. So, while you are praying and wishing to become a millionaire, all of Heaven is saying that it has already been placed inside of you. Your spirit has already received the seed and the millions of dollars. You already have it. Now you have to step out and do what God is telling you to do in order to manifest that seed in the natural and see your millions in your bank account.

God has so lovingly blessed you. Even with where you are now in life and what you currently have, you should begin to practice proper money management to prepare yourself for your increase. Be prepared for overflow before it arrives. Develop good habits with your finances and you will begin to prosper.

Principles to Steward Your Money Well

Keep in mind this key principle discussed earlier that **money cannot rule our lives or hearts**. It must have its rightful place in our lives.

Giving

This concept is difficult for many to understand but giving works like a seed. It produces a harvest. When you hold on to your money too tightly, it controls you. God has called you to rule and dominate. You must rule over your money with wisdom. A cheerful giver is a sign of someone who rules their money.

First, do not hold back God's tithe and offering. The Bible says that ten percent of all we make belongs to God. The government takes their cut, benefits, and everything else takes their share upfront, but we must honor God by giving Him what is His. It gives us an opportunity to put Him first. Jesus said that we should give the government what belongs to them and give to God what belongs to God.

> *"Render therefore to Caesar the things that are Caesar's, and to God the things that are God's."*
> *Matthew 22:21 (NKJV)*

> *" 'Bring all the tithes into the storehouse, that there may be food in My house, and try Me now in this,' says the Lord of hosts, 'If I will not open for you the windows of heaven and pour out for you such blessing that there will not be room enough to receive it.' "*
> *Malachi 3:10 (NKJV)*

God Himself is speaking in this passage. He commands us to bring the tithe, which is exactly 10% of our entire income, into His house so there is provision in the House of God. He said to try Him. The Bible says that we should not test God, but this is the one place God Himself makes an exception. He said to prove Him in this, test Him and see what He will do for you if you will commit to tithing. Since the tithe is a tenth of income, it means you tithe on the gross, not the net. The net is what you receive after the government and everyone else takes their cut. The gross is your total income before taxes or anything else is taken out. You must tithe on the gross because it is the total of your earnings.

I remember the story of a woman I knew who got saved. As a new Christian, she learned the principle of tithing and began doing it. Before her salvation and tithing, her husband's paycheck was not enough to carry her and her family through the month and she was unemployed due to an illness. They had to decide which bill should be left unpaid each month and sometimes struggled to get groceries and other necessities. She stepped out in faith and tithed, although things were tight. So, what happened? Her husband did not get a raise, at least not right away. More money was not flowing into their home, at least not right away. His income all of a sudden was now lasting them the entire month and a surplus was leftover. He was making the same amount as before and their expenses were the same. Miraculously, all their bills were paid monthly, they bought everything they needed and still had money left over. This is the miracle of tithing. God's math cannot be computed on a calculator but somehow it works!

I can share hundreds of stories about people who have tithed and reaped great benefits. From millionaires to seemingly average people, there are numerous testimonies of them consistently reaping blessings as a result of their dedication to tithing. It always benefits us to obey God. His Word is given for our benefit. It keeps the enemy away and keeps us under His covering. When we fail to tithe, we open up our finances to the devourer, who can operate in our finances and "eat" our money away. This is why God spoke through the prophet Malachi and said that He will rebuke the devourer when we tithe. Remember that the tithe is 10%. If you give less, you are not tithing.

Several people over the centuries have experimented with tithing. A pastor shared this story with me regarding someone he knew. He was a wealthy man who decided to experiment with tithing, and he claimed that his income more than doubled. It did not make logical sense, so he attributed it to tithing. He then continued tithing and giving well above the ten percent and his income grew so much that he had more money than he knew what to do with. He ended up giving 90% to God and charity and keeping only 10% for himself. I believe as a result of his tithing and his faith in reaping, God gave him increased wisdom. This duo built overflowing wealth for him.

There was another experiment from a couple who attends a local church. They had been saved for years but did not regularly practice tithing. They decided to give it a try. They realized that tithing improved their marriage because it taught them how to give and to consider others before themselves; it disciplined them and provided benefits that were not financial. They grew as people. They also had more peace, were happier, and made greater progress in life, living with more meaning and purpose than in the past. Now, they did receive financial blessings. First, they noticed that their money stretched further than it did in the past. Later, their monthly income increased and continued to increase. They reaped the benefits of tithing and realized that God really does reward those who give.

Outside of the tithe, we can give offerings to God according to our income, as well as giving to charities. The tithe is His no matter what, but offerings depend on whether or not you have it to give. Take care of your family and your bills and if you have extra, you can give an offering to bless the church, a ministry, a minister, or a charitable organization. Jesus sharply rebuked the Scribes and Pharisees for teaching the people to take money that should be given to their parents (to help take care of them) and instead bring it to the "Church." He called them hypocrites. (Matthew 15:1-9). God expects us to take care of our responsibilities and the people in our care. Again, this does not include the tithe. The tithe is God's no matter what and should not be used for any purpose other than the work of God. Your offering comes out of your "extra" income and is given at your own free will because you know giving pleases God. He will bless you for your giving and sacrifice.

As a disclaimer, if the Holy Spirit leads you to give, no matter the amount, you have to be obedient and just give it. He knows what He is doing and loves to reward us for our obedience. So in a situation like this where God is telling you to give, do not focus on how the sacrifice hurts, but on the blessing you are being to others and on how great your God rewards.

God wants us to be a blessing to other people. He blessed Abraham and told him that He would make him a blessing (Genesis 12:2). In him, *"all nations of the earth will be blessed"* (Genesis 12:3). God is a God of community. He expects us to be good Samaritans of each other and take care of those around us in need. When it comes to your local church or a ministry that you trust, you do not need to pray to ask God to give. I find that oftentimes people do this when they do not want to give. The Bible instructs us to give so we already know that it is the will of God.

I find that many Christians think of only giving to the Church. Giving to charity, other believers, and to the poor is very important to God. When it comes to charitable giving, be careful whom you give to. Be led by the Holy Spirit as some charities may have ethical and spiritual conflicts. For example, I like to select charities with low administrative fees, where I know most of my donation is going to the cause and not in the CEO's pocket. Also, some charities support satanic causes, so be very careful that you are not funding the work of the enemy.

I recall being pregnant with my first child and went for several months without being able to drink water. It made me sick each time I had any water. It was terrible. Before pregnancy, I loved drinking water and drank ten cups each day. It felt brutal to not be able to drink water and substitute for other forms of hydration. Finally, I reached a point where I could drink it and I rejoiced immensely in the house. My wonderful husband said to me that I should consistently donate to a charity that provides water to those who do not have access to it. He said that I had a small taste of their misery so I should partner with a charity doing this work to help the people who are suffering even worse than I had to suffer. After having our son, I forgot about the conversation and moved on. Then one night, God spoke to me in a dream and reminded me of the words of my husband. God wanted me to give. He loves giving and His Hand is moved to bless those who are cheerful givers. I obeyed and currently give to Water for Life, a charity run by James and Betty Robison. It has been such a blessing in my life to release that seed each time.

Did you know that when the Bible speaks of being a cheerful giver, it means to give while laughing hilariously? Some scholars depict this as laughing like a hyena. It is funny when you think about it, and I am not suggesting that you laugh like a hyena when giving your offering in Church (although it would be funny to see). But I am suggesting that you laugh within your heart. Have an attitude of rejoicing and laughter when you are giving.

We discussed earlier how God loves and honors His offering and He expects the same of us. Here are some tips I try to live by, based on what God has taught me over several years.

1. Give the tithe, which is 10%. Anything less than 10% is not the tithe. I round up, just to be safe.

2. Give the tithe first. Before bills are paid, before any money is spent from that paycheck, separate God's tithe and set it apart for Him. This leads to my next point.

3. Pray over and offer the tithe to God right away. I do not wait until I am in Church. I pray to God and tell Him that I am offering Him His tithe. I read the Scripture in Malachi 3:10-12 and praise God for the blessings He promises me as a result of tithing. Sometimes, I attach it to a more specific expectation, that is, I ask God for some specific blessing in my life. I worship Him and offer Him

the tithe at home. Only after doing this do I feel comfortable spending anything from my paycheck whether on bills, groceries, or anything else. If I am giving my tithe as a check, then before I begin this act of offering up the tithe to God, the check is written and set aside for God. I will put it in the offering basket when I go to church. If I am giving electronically such as via a website or app on my phone, I then go ahead and give the tithe at home after I am done offering it to God in prayer. Once it is separated and offered to God you absolutely cannot touch it or use it for personal use. That would be a severe dishonor to God's offering, as we discussed earlier with Eli and his sons.

4. Always honor God's tithe and offering. He takes it very seriously and so should we. Do not forget to give Him the tithe. Do not be one of those people who get to church and are scrambling for money to give in the offering. It shows that we disregard the offering of God. Rather, come to church prepared with your offering to give. Giving to God is a form of worship.

"And you shall love the Lord your God with all your heart, with all your soul, with all your mind, <u>and with all your strength</u>. This is the first commandment."
Mark 12:30 (NKJV)

Giving to God from our finances is how we love Him with our strength. Our money comes from our labor and when we give Him a portion of it, we give Him something that matters very much to us. It shows that we love Him more than money because we give much-needed money away to Him, in order to walk in obedience. To tithe consistently means that your heart is in the right place and that you love God more than you love money. Those who know to tithe and do not do it have an issue in their hearts. Money is glorified so highly in their hearts that they are unable to part from it, even when God is asking them to. Money becomes more important than God Himself, and therefore, money becomes their god. Mammon is the name of the god of money. The Scripture below makes it clear – you must decide if Jesus is your God, or if you will serve money instead. You will not be able to serve both.

"You cannot serve God and mammon"
Matthew 6:24 (NKJV)

While I could continue writing on giving, that topic is worthy of a book all by itself. Let us move further into other important principles to rule over your money well and establish a good relationship with your finances as a good steward of Jesus Christ.

Reduce Your Expenses

Get to know your expenses and take control of them. To build wealth, it is so important that you control your expenses and reduce your spending. A wealthy person who does not control their expenses well, can end up in a lot of debt and lose their wealth. We have seen this in the media where someone becomes a celebrity making millions of dollars but then a few years go by and they are on video flipping burgers at a fast-food restaurant. It takes discipline to be a good steward over your expenses. Also, you sometimes may have to embrace the concept of delayed gratification. All that means is you deny yourself certain pleasures now so that you can get to a better place in life and enjoy greater pleasures later.

When I graduated from college, I knew I would get married in a few years. As you know by now, I am a dreamer and I dreamt for years of a lavish wedding. Right away I worked hard to save. I denied myself the spending that many of my peers were doing and saved instead. I cut out unnecessary shopping, eating out, and other activities. I was diligent about saving. Any extra income that came into my life went directly into savings after the tithe and offering were given to God. My husband, who was my boyfriend at the time, proposed, I said yes and went on to plan my dream wedding. I had the wedding of my dreams and I do not regret spending the money for it. I sacrificed and denied myself things that I wanted to get a much bigger blessing down the road. This is how delayed gratification works. The sacrifice is worth it because you end up better off in the end. Our wedding was a huge blessing from God. He gave me the desires of my heart for my wedding and I give Him all the glory. Just like He did that for me, there is so much more He can do for you as well. Trust Him and He will give you your heart's longings.

Let me clarify and add my disclaimer here that I am not saying couples should spend all their money on their wedding. You have to know and do what works for your situation. I knew that I would never regret having an expensive wedding. It was similar to a bucket list item for me – it was a dream of mine and I wanted it fulfilled. I knew at the time that God was going to make me wealthy and He wanted me to have my heart's desires. So, we went for it!

Search your life. Find areas of unnecessary spending. If you are doing this as a couple do not focus on the other person – focus on you. It may hurt but list the things that you can sacrifice now to save more money and build a better future. Even the smallest changes count, so do not belittle any avenue to savings. It will feel rewarding and exciting to see the extra income in your bank account, especially as it keeps on steadily growing. This process can sometimes feel challenging so keep reminding yourself *why* you are making these sacrifices. They are not for nothing but to help discipline you so that when more income flows into your life, you know how to manage it. If you can prove your ability to properly manage what you currently own, then God will trust you with more and more and even more.

Budget

Budgets are very important. I have been budgeting since high school when I worked as a cashier at a home store. A budget gives you a sense of accountability, it sets goals for you and most importantly, it paints a clear picture of your finances. People in all income brackets should have a budget, from the poorest to the wealthiest. Learning to budget now makes it much easier to be a good manager of your money when God blesses you with wealth. As you are preparing for your riches, the budgeting process allows you to develop the correct financial disciplines so when you are wealthy, you already possess the skills to properly use and allocate your money and to be overall smarter with it.

Here are a few tips on creating a successful budget.

- Have a "why" behind your budget. Know why you are doing this so that when it gets hard, you have the motivation to keep pressing forward.

- Be realistic. If it is too difficult to follow, it just might not work. I will admit that there are times when I do set an aggressive budget but I know that I have the discipline to pull it off, which leads to my next point.

- Stick to it. A budget is defeated by your lack of discipline, so stick to your budget.

- Keep the end goal in mind. I always set a savings goal for my budget – how much do you want to save this year? Break it down into smaller, monthly chunks then see where you can cut back to achieve that goal. You can also reverse this method and instead of starting with an end savings goal, you can determine how much you can cut out each month, and that automatically becomes your savings goal. Either way, you end up saving more money than you would have before, so it is a win! Budgeting is a sign of wisdom. When God takes you into more financial prosperity, this type of wisdom will help ensure you do not lose your wealth.

- Hold yourself accountable. Do not make excuses if you fall off budget, especially if it is done repeatedly. At the same time, I do not want you to agonize over mistakes. Focus on getting back on track immediately.

- Reward yourself! As you make progress, give yourself small rewards to help you keep momentum. Treat yourself to something nice after you have reached a savings goal or milestone.

- Use a budgeting app or website. It makes it so much easier to budget. I hear impressive things about Mint[6], although I have not used it myself and I am not affiliated with it.

- PRAY ABOUT IT! Always pray about everything. Talk to God about your plans. Let Him know how much you want to save and ask Him to help you. Let Him know your weaknesses and ask for His grace and wisdom. It takes wisdom to build wealth, so pray to God for wisdom every day. God will even show you areas in your life where you can save money that you might not have thought about before.

- You will want to assess your budget and expenses periodically to see if there are further tweaks needed, and there will be. God is getting ready to prosper you so your budget numbers will change.

Right now, you may be budgeting in the hundreds and the thousands but imagine the day when you will be budgeting in the tens of thousands, hundreds of thousands, and millions. Selah!

Savings

A general rule of thumb is to save 20% of your after-tax income. However, this does not work for everyone. You may not have the capacity to save as much as 20% and there may be others who are able to go above 20%. If you are not able to save 20% or more, then reassess your spending and budget every few months to determine if there are more areas you have discovered that you can cut back on and increase savings. Work towards getting to 20% at a pace that feels right for your circumstance. The idea is to continually push yourself to save more and more and more.

With all that money that you are now saving, keep at least three months of expenses in a high yield savings account such as a money market account. My preference is six months but experts like Dave Ramsey[7] and others set three months as the minimum. This is in case an emergency arises or you lose your job. It ensures that you have a cushion to fall back on.

Now, wealthy people focus more on investing than saving. I believe that before arriving at wealth, we must learn to save to be prepared for unpredictable things in the future. Saving creates another discipline, like reducing expenses and budgeting, that helps us to be more successful as we continue to grow financially. When God brings you into wealth, be sure to work with a wealth management firm that has a good reputation to help reassess how much you should save and how much you should invest. Keep in mind that I said a wealth management firm *with a good reputation*.

Save for Retirement

Many look forward to the day they can retire. But how good will it be if you do not have enough saved up to sustain your life? Now, you might be thinking that you are on your way to becoming a millionaire so you do not need a retirement account. And you are right but here me out – a retirement acts as an additional form of investment, presenting you an opportunity to gain interest and to also receive additional money from your current employer in the form of a match. Additionally, there are some of you who want to find success and prosperity working for a company as opposed to having 100% of your income come from entrepreneurship. You are called to be leaders at various companies, bringing the Kingdom of God there and rising to success with the help of God. Your retirement account will benefit you greatly. I advise you to have one, even after you become wealthy.

Typically, it is advised to save 10 – 15% of your pre-tax income into a retirement account. If your employer offers a 401K, please take advantage of the full match. I repeat – invest in your 401K because your employer gives you money for doing so. It is free money! Take advantage of the highest match they offer. Speak with human resources to learn as much as you can about how the plan works and take full advantage of it. Do not flush that free money down the toilet.

You may not be able to afford to put 10 – 15% of your income into retirement but consider gradually increasing the amount until you have arrived at the 10 – 15% mark. If you are in your twenties, aiming for 10% is sufficient. For someone in their 30's and older, it is more important to get closer to the 15% mark to reach your retirement goals. Once you have reached the legal limit of investing in your 401K, consider moving on to a Roth IRA. 401Ks are pre-tax so you do not pay taxes on them now, but you do when you withdraw the money in retirement. Roth IRAs on the other hand are post taxes and are not taxed when you withdraw from your retirement account in the future. I do love that about the IRA. When you retire and withdraw from your account, you do not have to worry about paying taxes.

I recommend speaking with a financial advisor to get the best advice for your specific situation. They will tailor their recommendation to your individual goals, income, risk tolerance, and age. If you are self-employed, you can skip to the Roth IRA but work with a financial planner/advisor. Do not overlook retirement. Take a selah moment and take this seriously. Most people are not prepared to retire. We know that God will take care of us and that He is our Provider, but He gives us wisdom. It is wise to plan for your retirement and your future in general.

The Bible teaches the importance of putting provision away for the future. Solomon, who is considered the wisest man to ever live, speaks of the ant who is so wise that it stores up food without being told, so it has provision for the winter (Proverbs 30:24-25). You can think of winter as retirement – it represents a time when the harvest slows down or is completely cut off. The ants are saving for their future. Having more than enough in storage will get you through your winter seasons without worry. Even millionaires have storages of money designated for specific dates in the future. Trust funds also can operate this way, where they are saved and collect interest. Some have stipulations that the money cannot be withdrawn until a certain date.

The retirement information might not be for everyone but it is advice I often give and I find that many people in the Church do not have an understanding of retirement. I believe we have a duty to educate people on life as well. When you obtain your wealth and riches and you decide to forgo retirement savings, use wisdom to have a storage of money for the future that is sufficient to provide for years to come.

Invest

Invest invest invest! It is considered one of the best ways to build wealth. Investing has birthed countless millionaires. There are many rags to riches stories thanks to the stock market, other forms of investing, and some savvy investors. You may not be prepared to invest now, but as God increases your finances it is a good idea to invest at that time.

Never tackle this on your own. Whether you read articles that offer investment advice and specific investments to purchase, or you work with a certified investment professional, get help from a professional. Investing can be complicated and there is always the risk that you can lose money. When I first started investing, I used the Motley Fool[8] Stock Advisor service. I paid a small annual fee and they provided me with a list of stocks to invest in to create my first portfolio. It was very helpful and I highly recommend it for beginners. I also read articles on various business websites that helped provide guidance on investing and specific investments to purchase. I found that those articles were in agreement with the Motley Fool's[8] recommendations. Since then, many websites and apps have been created to help people of all ages invest better. Some include Robin Hood[9], Acorns[10], and Stash[11].

Robinhood[9] comes from the famous character who stole from the rich and gave to the poor. The app makes it cheaper for people to buy and sell on the stock market so everyone has access to that wealth. It has free stock trades so it works best for those who want a cheaper way to invest.

Acorns[10], as the name cleverly suggests, takes your extra change and invests it for you. It is the best option for those who want automated investing without having to do it themselves. It is linked to your financial account(s) and whenever you make purchases, Acorns rounds up the cost to the next dollar amount and invests the change. That way, with just about every purchase you make, your change gets invested. For some, that means they are investing every day without even thinking about it.

Stash[11] teaches you about investing so that you can make investment decisions yourself. You can build your portfolio from scratch or use their recommendations. Similar to Acorns, it has a feature to invest your money automatically but that is optional. If you want to learn more about investing and be more involved in the process, Stash might be best for you.

I must say that I am in no way affiliated with any of the companies aforementioned. I am just letting you know what I did and how it worked. I have friends and relatives who use Robinhood, Acorns, and Stash and they recommend them. You can also skip the apps altogether and use an investment advisor. For some, that is the easiest option as a real person is there to guide you throughout the entire process. Again, please do not just give your money to a random person - use a reputable firm.

Education

A key way to prosper in your field is to become more educated, which increases your qualifications and potentially your income. Furthering your education also means that more opportunities are available to you. You can widen your career opportunities and have more negotiating power. Whether you are an entrepreneur or not, furthering your education can help propel you forward.

With the tools the world recognizes such as education, and the abundant favor of God on your life, even more doors will open for you. God's favor will go before you and make ways for you. His favor will present you with greater opportunities. Recognize this –you are a child of God. He is for you and He is on your side. According to Isaiah 43:19b, He will *"make a way in the wilderness and rivers in the desert." (NKJV).* God knows how to use your education to open doors and advance you in this world. Have faith in Him.

Education is important but you should keep in mind that learning does not always happen in school. By reading this book, you have invested in your education. There are many avenues to learning including reading, watching educational videos, and going back to school. I want to emphasize this point – school and education do not give you your gifts. You came to Earth with them inside you already. Education sharpens your skills and refines your gifts.

An example of this is someone who loves making processes more efficient and overall improving things. This is the kind of person that has an opinion on how to change everything and some people may find them annoying. Let us assume that this person's gift is to improve processes for companies and help them run a more efficient operation – this is what God has called them to do to earn an income.

Well, they could complete the LEAN certification process, which qualifies them to review companies and change their operations for the better. With this qualification, they can become a consultant. Through dedication to this effort, they can become the leading consultant in this area and grow their consulting practice into other areas as well.

Whatever field you operate in, whether as a business owner or an employee, learn continuously. Find trusted resources you can use so you are kept up to date on happenings in your field and to increase your knowledge and expertise. This will boost your confidence and help drive you forward. Learn the industry that you want to succeed in. Understand how that market works, what customers value, industry trends, weaknesses, strengths, opportunities that have not yet been tapped, problems that currently exist, current and future challenges, changes in the industry, the technology impacting that industry, and more.

The Scriptures teach us that in all the things we get, be sure to get understanding (Proverbs 4:7). We spend time and money to obtain food, clothing, and to do so much more. God says to be sure that learning and understanding are included on your shopping list. Invest the time and money to increase your learning.

I will inject that not everyone has the opportunity to go back to school and that is okay. Do not feel down about that. Do what you can – invest in books to read, learn online, etc. God is more than able to bless you in your current situation. He already has everything that you need to prosper lined up for you and waiting on you. Just have faith.

Entrepreneurship

I love this one! Within each and every one of us is a gift and the ability to do something that benefits others in such a way that no one else can. You were designed to be on Earth at this time to release that gift into the world. We are taught to go to school, do well, land a good job, and work until it is time to retire. Well, that model does not always work and I somewhat disagree with it for you. Just going to work every day and waiting to retire is not fulfilling. You are powerful and have great things to accomplish. If you choose to be an employee because you love it and find it helps you fulfill your purpose, then I recommend still pursuing entrepreneurship as a part-time opportunity to go deeper into your purpose and to build wealth. Your job is not designed to make you rich, so you should couple entrepreneurship with it.

The bottom line is you have something you can do so well, others are willing to pay you for it. You have an idea that will make someone's life easier, and they are willing to give cash in exchange for it. Think of how you spend your money. You are simply buying other people's ideas that help make your life easier. You give them cash in exchange for their product or service. Now it is your turn to be on the receiving end.

For some, entrepreneurship will begin with their own strength and skill. For others, it is seizing an opportunity. For example, someone might love photography and it is easy to decide on launching a photography business. But for some, there is no clear skillset or interest. Instead, you find a problem that you can provide a solution to. You find an opportunity that leads way to a business. Many businesses started as someone's response to a problem, such as creating a new product or service that they needed but was not available on the market; or a feature needed in an existing product that they add and make it their own. They tap into a market that did not exist before.

Take for example Tara Williams of Dreamland Baby. I had the privilege of speaking with Tara, who started her company out of a need. She needed a weighted blanket for her baby to help him sleep. To her surprise, no such thing was on the market. So what did she do? She created one and turned it into a successful, seven-figure business. You can do the same. It is worth noting that Tara's business became a million-dollar business in just one year! It is your turn and with God, nothing can stop you.

You too have an idea inside of you. You have something that has been nagging away at you. No matter what you do, it just is not leaving you. Your seed is tugging away at your heart. Your ideas want to be birthed. Your vision wants to become your reality. Everyone has entrepreneurship inside of them. The Holy Spirit places it inside us all before we are even born.

The challenge many face is deciding on what to do. Some of you have clear ideas and visions while others are the same as I was. You know you want to do something great but you are not sure what. You may have many ideas but are not sure where to start. Ask The Holy Spirit to reveal to you what He wants you to do. Ask Him for wisdom in this area. He will speak to your heart and show you the path to take. Most often I find it is that one idea that has not left you. This often is the Holy Spirit speaking to you. He is bringing it to your mind.

You can also find that one great idea to start with. You know that one that has been on your mind since you were a child. The one thing you just cannot escape. Again, this could be God speaking to you. All your ideas will come to pass but you just need to pick one to get started with. Do not tackle all your ideas at once.

You should also learn the field you are launching into. God expects us to operate in wisdom. Do not just dive out of the plane without understanding how your parachute works. Learn the industry, your competitors, what customers value, and much more. You absolutely have what it takes to be a successful entrepreneur. Do not discourage yourself. Go forward with God on your side. You do not have to start as a full-time entrepreneur. You can do this part-time while you work your day job and eventually transition into full-time entrepreneurship when your business grows. As I mentioned before, some people love their careers and want to continue being an employee. I advise them to venture into entrepreneurship as a side income because we never want to put all our eggs in one basket.

Side note – remember what you just read on retirement? If your entrepreneurial ventures are your primary source of income, then also consider having a retirement account through your business. After all, eventually, you hope to pass this business down to the next generation and spend your remaining time traveling the world and lounging on your yacht (smiley face inserted here).

Do not forget to head over to the Workbook to complete your personal exercises for this chapter. Have fun with this one.

CHAPTER 7

Wealth's Greatest Secret

"My people are destroyed for lack of knowledge" Hosea 4:6 (NKJV)

Come to know and understand the key to building wealth. It is not to obtain more money – many have made money and lost it all. It is not to have a brilliant idea – many brilliant ideas are in the grave. It is not to be lucky – many lucky people have had their luck run out. There is one secret that the Bible makes evident as the pathway and the door to wealth and riches in unlimited abundance... and that is *obedience*. This is probably not the answer that many were expecting but as you walk through this chapter, you will understand why obedience is the secret to attaining wealth.

The entire summation of our Christian faith is to trust in God with no doubt and to obey Him. Faith and obedience work together and you will see this as you continue reading this chapter. I have come to the revelation that the answer to everything in life is to trust and obey God. The old saints sang,

"Trust and obey
for there is no other way
to be happy in Jesus
but to trust and obey."

They were so right! In everything we have faced and could ever face if we simply put our trust in God completely, have no doubt in Him, and obey everything He tells us to do, then nothing could ever stop, block or hinder us. Nothing could ever hurt us. The entire army of the devil can rise against us but if we keep our trust in God and follow His instructions, we will escape every snare and will be unharmed.

Faith and obedience go hand in hand because faith in God leads us to obey Him. Oftentimes we have ideas that we do not act upon simply because we do not believe that they will lead to success – we have some doubts. But when we put our faith in God, we have the confidence to step out and do the things He tells us to because we just know that it will all work out well. Deuteronomy chapter 4 explains how special we are because we have God Himself so near to us and He is fighting for us. With God on your side, who can rise against you and win? No one.

The Israelites were freed from Egypt, the land of their bondage. They wandered in the wilderness, the bridge between bondage and prosperity. They were in the wilderness for forty years but God really intended for it to take less than two weeks. Why did it take so much longer than it should have? They would not trust God. When God said to go in and possess the land, they were afraid and did not obey God. Fear took hold of them and instead of trusting and obeying God, they believed they were not strong enough and they were not good enough. They did not have faith in God, and they disobeyed. Keep in mind that it was their lack of faith that led to their disobedience. God was angry with them. They looked at the enemy who was in the land and thought the enemy would be too strong for them. They called themselves grasshoppers but forgot that God Almighty was fighting for them. Instead of looking to the power of God and His ability, knowing that He would definitely keep His promise to them, they doubted and looked at their own capability. They saw that they were inadequate and decided to remain stagnant instead of going forward and doing what God told them to do.

Whose heart am I speaking to? How many times have you stopped yourself from doing something that God told you to do because you looked at yourself or the situation and forgot how great your God truly is? You lost faith and disobeyed. The problem is God had already given them the land. He had already given them wealth and riches. They simply had to step out and obey Him in order to possess or to take hold of it in the natural. When God makes you a promise it is done and completed. He has given it to you in the realm of the spirit because God is a Spirit. Everything He does and gives to you occurs in the spirit realm. Your faith and obedience transcend it from the spirit to the natural. The only thing that can stop it from manifesting in the natural realm is your disobedience, and remember that disobedience comes from a lack of faith.

> *"Therefore I say to you, whatever things you ask when you pray, believe that you receive them, and you will have them."*
> *Mark 11:24 (NKJV)*

So you see according to Jesus' words in Mark, when you make a request to God in prayer, you must first know without a shadow of a doubt that God has answered and you have received of Him your requests. Only then will you actually have it. Your faith makes it your reality.

The Scripture makes it clear:

> *"Praise the Lord!*
> *Blessed is the man who fears the Lord,*

> *Who delights greatly in His commandments.*
> *His descendants will be mighty on earth;*
> *The generation of the upright will be blessed.*
> *Wealth and riches will be in his house,*
> *And his righteousness endures forever."*
> *Psalm 112:1-3 (NKJV)*

Those who fear God and enjoy His commandments and instructions will be mighty on earth and wealth and riches will be in their house. This Scripture clearly tells us that wealth and riches are a direct fruit of obedience to God.

Through obedience, you enter a place of rest, or what Scripture calls the rest of God.

God created rest for the children of Israel.

*"And to the Reubenites, the Gadites, and half the tribe of Manasseh Joshua spoke, saying, 'Remember the word which Moses the servant of the Lord commanded you, saying, '**The Lord your God is giving you rest and is giving you this land.**' Your wives, your little ones, and your livestock shall remain in the land which Moses gave you on this side of the Jordan. But you shall pass before your brethren armed, all your mighty men of valor, and help them, **until the Lord has given your brethren rest, as He gave you, and they also have taken possession of the land which the Lord your God is giving them. Then you shall***

return to the land of your possession and enjoy it, which Moses the Lord's servant gave you on this side of the Jordan toward the sunrise.'"
Joshua 1:12-15 (NKJV)

I became excited when I first saw the revelation in this passage of Scripture, that the rest God promised is the promised land. Joshua told the first two and a half tribes that God had given them rest but that they should help the remaining tribes to fight until they have received their rest, that is until they have taken possession of their promised land. And then God instructs them to return to their promised land and ENJOY IT! Our place of rest is meant to be enjoyed.

The rest of God means that they would cease from their toil and hard labor. They would be able to live out their dream life and be happy doing so. When you are in the rest of God, it means that you have arrived at the place of your destiny. You are whom He has called you to be, doing what He desires of you. You are no longer trying to get to a certain place in life – you have already arrived there. The rest of God is when you are living your dream life. You have the marriage and family He desires for you; your career and business are successful and satisfying; you are doing exactly what you are called to do and feeling great about it; your finances are overflowing with abundance; you are in good health; everything around you is productive and multiplying and there are no enemies in sight; you are dwelling in peace and happiness. The rest of God, the rest He promised in the Scripture, is the promised land. The promised land is your dream life.

This was the plan of God for the Israelites – for them to enter His rest. He wanted it so desperately for them, but they would not obey Him nor would they trust Him. Instead, they wandered in the wilderness until that generation died and their children took possession of the promised land. I observed in the Scripture that the generation that died in the wilderness was raised in Egypt. They were from the land of bondage and had the mindset of bondage. Although they saw God do so many wonders and miracles right before their faces, they struggled to continually trust Him because they still had the wrong mindset. The moment something went wrong, they worried and complained. They always assumed that something bad was going to happen to them. When they became thirsty in the wilderness, instead of thinking, "God is so powerful. We saw the miracles He did with the waters in Egypt so we know that He will provide water for us to drink," they thought that God brought them to the wilderness to let them die. They did not know Him nor did they have a revelation of His love for them. As a result of their inability to grasp how deeply He loved them and wanted the best for them, they always assumed that at the first sign of trouble it meant that God was punishing them or something bad was about to happen to them.

How sad is this mindset and the reality is that many Christians today think like this. Because they were so accustomed to being mistreated by the Egyptians, they approached God with that same mindset. Please understand that God is not the same as that parent that rejected you, the spouse that used you, the friend that betrayed you; He is not just around you for what He can get from you nor will He turn His back on you when you make a mistake. He loves you and nothing can change that. He will take your hand and walk you along your journey in life every step of the way. If you make a mistake, repent right away. He will simply take you by the hand and show you the correct way in love, kindness, and patience. HE IS FOR YOU! Repeat that to yourself every day. God is for you and He will never harm you. Everything He asks you to do is for your benefit and prosperity.

The generation that did enter the promised land was raised by Joshua. They did not have the mindset of bondage from Egypt. They were taught about God and His power so they knew to trust in Him. Unfortunately, their parents could not shed the old mindset to trust God and inherit their blessings. It took forty years for them to travel from the land of bondage to the promised land because that was the length of time needed for the generation who would not trust and obey God to die. Because of their incorrect mindset, God could not bless them.

We discussed mindset in chapter 1 but I hope that you are seeing here how important the right thinking is to your destiny. It is so important that if we do not think right, it can hinder us from possessing our possessions and taking all that God has for us.

Here is what Hebrews says about the generation that died in the wilderness:

"For who, having heard, rebelled? Indeed, was it not all who came out of Egypt, led by Moses? Now with whom was He angry forty years? Was it not with those who sinned, whose corpses fell in the wilderness? And to whom did He swear that they would not enter His rest, but to those who did not obey? So we see that they could not enter in because of unbelief." Hebrews 3:16-19 (NKJV)

This is the generation we are speaking of. It explains that God swore that they would not enter the promised land because they did not obey but the next line says that they could not enter because of unbelief. So you see, unbelief and "did not obey" are used interchangeably here because **unbelief and disobedience are the same thing.** When you doubt God, you are actually disobeying Him. Unbelief, or a lack of faith, causes us to harden our hearts and anything God speaks after that becomes difficult for us to obey.

Hebrews then says this:

> *"Since therefore it remains that some must enter it, and those to whom it was first preached **did not enter because of disobedience**, again He designates a certain day, saying in David, 'Today,' after such a long time, as it has been said: 'Today, if you will hear His voice, Do not harden your hearts.'"*
>
> *Hebrews 4:6-7 (NKJV)*

You see that they did not enter their promised land because of disobedience, so God warns the next generations, cautioning them to be prepared to obey the voice of God. Prepare your heart ahead of time to obey His instructions. This is how you enter your rest, your promised land – when you obey Him. If you hear Him speak, in any way or form, do not harden your heart. Do not become stubborn. Do not fall victim to reasoning and making sense of everything. Do not try to analyze it and come up with a plan. Do not think your way is best because you are not the Sovereign God. Your one ask, your one task, is to simply obey. This is what He asks and requires of us. Should you hear His voice, should He move your heart in a direction, should He drop an inspiring thought in your mind, simply obey and do so right away.

Take a moment now and be sure that you are released from the wrong thinking you have adopted from your past bondage, your upbringing, family, friends, culture, surroundings, etc. You should know that God loves you and will never hurt you no matter what! You should always believe that He has your best interest at heart.

This is the key to trusting God. You know that He sees more than you see so when He says "go left" although you don't know what is waiting for you around the corner, you just trust that God knows and it has to be good because everything He has for you is good. Do not fall into the trap of that generation. They never saw the promised land. They never experienced their wealth and riches. Trust in God. You do not need to understand. You do not need any details. Just trust Him and do what He says. God wants to make your dreams come true, but you have to trust and obey Him, otherwise, you will die in the wilderness and never see your promised land.

Prepare your heart to obey Him. Repeat to yourself daily, that if you hear His voice you will not harden your heart, as the Scripture instructs. If you prepare yourself, then it is easier to obey when He speaks.

Becoming a mom has taught me so much from the perspective of God. My children at times want certain things that I am happy to give them but their behavior can delay and sometimes deny them the very things they want. A common example is when my son wants to go to the playground. I try to get him dressed and put on his shoes so we can leave but instead he starts goofing off. He then keeps wondering why we have not left the house for the park. I tell him, "If you will just do as I tell you to, you will have exactly what you want and you'll get it sooner."

Another example is my daughter. She wants me to nurse her but at times I know that she will fall asleep. So I decide to change her diaper before feeding her so that she is comfortable while sleeping. Well, little missy (as I often call her) decides to kick and scream because I am not feeding her right away. How dare I not give her what she wants when she wants it – that is probably what she is thinking. All that kicking and screaming makes the process take much longer. When I finally get the diaper on after several tries, putting her clothes back on is another battle. If she would simply submit to my process, she would still get exactly what she wants and be happier the whole way through. She gets an extra blessing as well because she can sleep more comfortably and not squirm in a wet diaper. This has shown me the importance of submitting to God. We tend to doubt and fight God when we do not understand. We throw a tantrum when things do not go our way and He just wants us to submit to His process. Whatever He is doing is best for us. It is to help us and to make us prosper. Instead of trusting when we do not understand, we fight and try to find ways to make things happen ourselves. Friends, this only delays your progress and sometimes creates another mess that God has to clean up. Make up in your mind today to submit to Him no matter what.

At times, we are not able to connect the dots of God. You pray for a beautiful house or to obtain riches but God responds by placing an idea in your mind or He instructs you to start a business in a field where you have little to no experience. We are not able to see how doing what God tells us to do will give us what we want in the future. God responds to faith. He will not give you all the details or show you a clear roadmap. Instead, He expects you to trust Him. He expects you to act as though you know Him because to know God is to trust Him. This is why the book of Romans states that faith comes by hearing the Word of God (Romans 10:17). The more you learn the Word, the more you get to know God, and the more you know Him the more you trust Him. For some people, the more you get to know them the more you realize you cannot trust them. But because God is so Awesome and His love for you is so deep and unmeasurable, the more you learn of Him, the more you realize how silly you were to walk in fear and doubt, and you begin to trust Him more and more. He will direct you to take a step where there is no road and expect that, because you know He loves you, you will have the confidence that He will not let you fall. Somehow, when you take that step, you just believe that you will not fall.

I hope by now you are seeing the connection between obedience and the manifestation of your wealth. Obedience is the path to your promised land and in your promised land is all the wealth and riches you can imagine.

Obedience is your path to prosperity.

Do you need more evidence? Let us look at Moses.

Moses, the servant of God who led the children of Israel out of bondage did not enter the promised land. But the real question is why? In Numbers chapter twenty, we see the story of the Israelites, where they were thirsty and complaining about water. God instructs Moses and Aaron to speak to the rock Meribah so that it brings forth water. Instead, since Moses and Aaron were angry with the Israelites, they struck the rock twice and it brought forth water. They did not speak to it and therefore the miracle of God was not performed. The people did not get to see the Hand of God at work. God responds in verse twelve and tells them that as a result of this disobedience, they will not enter the promised land.

> "Then the Lord spoke to Moses and Aaron, "Because you did not believe Me, to hallow Me in the eyes of the children of Israel, therefore you shall not bring this assembly into the land which I have given them." Numbers 20:12 (NKJV)

God speaks of their disobedience and says that they did not believe Him. Here too, God is showing us that unbelief is disobedience. They were angry with the people and therefore began operating in the carnal nature. They were in the flesh, which is the breeding ground for doubt. Once doubt and unbelief developed in their hearts, it led to their disobedience. It cost them so much. Moses, the man who performed such great miracles and did such wonders before the people; the man who spent forty days and nights immersed in God's Presence, whose face shone so bright from the Glory of God that no one could look on it; this great man of God called Moses did not enter the promised land because He disobeyed.

> *"Because you trespassed [sinned] against Me among the children of Israel at the waters of Meribah Kadesh, in the Wilderness of Zin, because you did not hallow [honor] Me in the midst of the children of Israel. Yet you shall see the land before you, though you shall not go there, into the land which I am giving to the children of Israel."*
> *Deuteronomy 32:51-52 (NKJV)*

God told him that he would see the land, but not enter it.

You see, your title and your service do not guarantee your promised land – your obedience does.

Do not get hung up on your past disobedience. God is merciful that if you repent, He will forgive you. But makeup in your heart to stop repeating these same mistakes. You are delaying yourself from your blessings and your prosperity when you disobey.

Earlier, we saw that Abraham died a very wealthy man. But how did his wealth come? It did not just land in his lap all of a sudden. God gave him an instruction - to leave the land of his father and go to a foreign land that God will show him (Genesis 12). As Abraham, then known as Abram, followed the voice of God from place to place, He acquired wealth. Each place he went and each step of obedience brought blessings into his life until He prospered mightily. Abraham had several hundred servants. Can you imagine the amount of wealth and property he must have had to house that many servants?

As we discuss the topic of obedience, note that the most important thing is to be in right standing with God. Once you have established a relationship with Him, God will continually speak to you. He knows your dreams and your desires. He knows the destiny that He has placed inside of you. He will speak to you and give you instructions. He is constantly speaking to His children. He speaks to us every day even at night in our dreams. He gives us instructions to get through life. I hear God throughout the day telling me to "do this" or "don't say that" etc. If we will listen to Him and obey Him without fighting or trying to make sense of it, we will be much better off. You may not always see how His commandments and instructions connect with the big picture but just trust Him because He knows so much more than we do. As you obey the first instruction, He gives the second. When you obey the second command, He then reveals the third, and so on.

As you are reading this book, I believe that God is speaking to you. There are ideas that have come to you that God planted in your mind. You may have gotten a business idea from God. Well, get started on it. If you are waiting for God to give you all the details including the "whys" and "hows" you will be waiting forever. Get started on doing the little He has told you, then as you walk in obedience, He will provide more information to you. As you face decisions, He will speak and shed light on the right way to go. Remember, He is walking with you step by step as you establish your business or take on any venture to change your life. It is you and God doing it together.

"Every commandment which I command you today you must be careful to observe, that you may live and multiply, and go in and possess the land of which the Lord swore to your fathers."
Deuteronomy 8:1 (NKJV)

Be careful to obey every instruction of God. Do not miss even one. Also, do not delay in your obedience because you can miss the window of opportunity that God had lined up for you. Disobedience can cost you. In Numbers chapters thirteen and fourteen, God instructed the Israelites to take the land of Canaan, but the people became afraid. They were so afraid, they decided to remain where they were and not possess that land. They complained and God labeled it as rebellion and said that they were wicked. He said they are treating Him with hatred. Be careful not to complain. Be careful to trust God. The next day they changed their minds and decided to obey God. Well, it was too late. They missed the window of opportunity and lost that battle. Had they obeyed God when He spoke, they would have been victorious. Now, we know that God is merciful. While they lost that battle and their disobedience delayed them, it did not stop them completely. The Israelites still eventually defeated the enemy and took possession of that territory.

Are you tired of being delayed? Are you tired of wishing and hoping and wanting? Then there is no time for disobedience. Do what God says, when He says it, and how He says to. Do not miss one step. Trust Him completely. Remember that obedience is a product of trusting in God.

Keep faith in your heart. Meditate daily on the Word of God to build your faith. Remember to meditate on God's Word is to repeat it to yourself several times. It means to mutter it under your breath. The more you hear the Word, the more your faith rises and doubt departs from you.

> *"Behold the proud, His soul is not upright in him;*
> *But the just shall live by his faith." Habakkuk 2:4 (NKJV)*

The Bible makes it clear that the just shall live by his own faith. You live according to your faith. So if you have little faith, then you will live a little life. If you have mediocre faith, then you will be average. But if you have great faith, then you will build a great life and reap the fruits of greatness. Your background has no input nor does your family line matter. You do not need to come from greatness to be great. If you have great faith, then you will do great things.

As a child, my dad spoke over his children, "there is greatness inside of you." I heard this statement almost every day of my life until I became an adult and moved out. It was a seed planted in me and when I found myself not doing great things, I was ready to burst at the seams. It just did not feel right. Even if I wanted to, I could not stifle that seed. Well, I speak it over you today. THERE IS GREATNESS INSIDE OF YOU! Speak this over your life and your children daily.

Even when obstacles come your way, they are all part of the plan of God to get you to your blessing. In the book of Joshua chapter ten beginning at verse five, five Kings teamed up together to fight against Joshua and Israel's army. Joshua became concerned. In the past, God told him whom to launch an attack against and reassured him that he would win. This time, God did not first speak to Joshua and instruct him to fight these five nations. They chose to pursue and attack Joshua and they were mighty. Joshua went before God and God reassured him that He is with him and He is fighting for him. God gave Joshua a great victory that day and in the course of two days, he destroyed all their armies and completely defeated them. But the point I want to leave with you is that once Joshua was done, he now had five additional nations added to his inheritance in the span of two days. It seemed intimidating that they all came against him at once, but God turned it around for his good and it was a means of expediting his blessing. How would you like to receive five times your blessing all at once? You absolutely can but it comes by faith and obedience.

> *"Only be strong and very courageous, that you may observe to do according to all the law which Moses My servant commanded you; do not turn from it to the right hand or to the left, that you may prosper wherever you go. This Book of the Law shall not depart from your mouth, but you shall meditate in it day and night, that you may observe to do according to all that is written in It. For then you will make your way prosperous, and then you will have good success. Have I not commanded you? Be strong and of good courage; do not be afraid, nor be dismayed, for the Lord your God is with you wherever you go."*
>
> *Joshua 1:7-9 (NKJV).*

Let us examine the text above. After the death of Moses, God is speaking to Joshua, Moses' successor. He first tells him to be strong and very courageous, but why? So that he obeys the commandment Moses left behind. It takes courage to obey God. He will tell you to do things that do not make sense. Others may think you are crazy or that something is wrong with you. You most likely will not fit in with some people when you decide to walk in complete obedience to God. He will ask you to do things that make it difficult for you to connect the dots or understand. It takes courage to walk in obedience to God so today I tell you, just as God told Joshua before he began the journey to the promised land, be strong my friend, and be very courageous.

God then tells Joshua that he should not turn away from the Word of God – why? So that he will prosper *wherever he goes*. Do you want to prosper wherever you go and in everything you do? Obey God's Word without wavering. Obey the written word in the Bible but also the things He speaks to your heart. Obey every instruction – do not miss even one. When you do this, prosperity will find you because every command God gives you is a step on your path to prosper in life.

In verse eight, God gave more detail on how Joshua can consistently obey Him. He tells Him that the Word should never leave his mouth but that he should meditate on it day and night. Hearing the Word better empowers you to obey it. The world has its meditation which is rooted in satanism, but the Bible teaches that we should meditate on God's Word. If people would replace yoga and other forms of demonic "relaxation" and meditation with meditating on the Word of God, their hearts would overflow with peace and they would be more successful at overcoming all the problems they experience. God tells Joshua that if he meditates on the Word, then he will be empowered to obey it. Then, he will make his way prosperous and then he will have good success. If you will do the same, you too will reap the same benefits. Meditate on His Word day and night. This also prepares your heart so that when He speaks to you and instructs you, you are ready to obey Him.

Lastly in verse nine God so lovingly reassures Joshua that He is there for him. How wonderful Joshua must have felt to know that the God of the universe is with him, the One who is above all and holds all power. You and I have that privilege and more so. What is God telling you to do? What is that risk that you want to take? Know that He is with you. You are not alone and you are not forgotten. God is right by your side every step of the way. In fact, He went before you and prepared the way to your destiny and prosperity.

Your path to prosperity was prepared long before you were born. Now walk it in faith, knowing that God Almighty is on your side.

Please head over to the Workbook to complete your personal exercises for this chapter.

CHAPTER 8

The Destruction of Fear

"The Lord said to Joshua, 'Do not be afraid of them; I have given them into your hand. Not one of them will be able to withstand you.'"
Joshua 10:8 (NIV)

Fear is one of the most common tools the enemy uses to stop, block, and hinder many. It is crippling to its prey and has suffocated millions of dreams and ideas. I do not want this to be your fate. To enter your promised land, you must destroy fear. In the opening Scripture, Joshua ten, we see that God is speaking to Joshua letting him know that there is absolutely nothing to fear because God has already given them the promised land. There is no reason to be afraid of the armies they had to fight against to win the land because as far as God was concerned, the land was already theirs.

You do not have to be afraid to venture out and do what God has placed in your heart to do. God has already guaranteed that you will succeed and that all will be well with you. He has walked the path to your prosperity and has fought every demon you would face and crushed every obstacle that could dare stand in your way. Then He comes back, takes your hand, and instructs you to walk the same path. God has everything lined up for your success if you just follow His plan. Even people who dislike you will have to bless you if God wants them to.

I want you to understand that fear is not just a human emotion. Fear is a spirit.

> *"For God has not given us the **spirit of fear;**
> but of power, and of love, and of a sound mind.*
> *II Timothy 1:7 (NKJV)*

Since fear is a spirit and it is not from God, we can correctly call fear a demon - a spirit from satan. To fight against this demon, the text lists three things God has given to us.

First, God has given you power. This power lets you know that you have already overcome whatever it is you are afraid of. You have the power of God working in you and therefore, you have nothing to be afraid of. When fear shows up in your life, you can command it to leave. You have a power that is greater than fear. Exercise your God-given right and cast fear out of your life.

Second, God has given us a spirit of love. Love is absolutely powerful. The Bible says,

"There is no fear in love; but perfect love casts out fear, because fear involves torment. But he who fears has not been made perfect in love."
I John 4:18 (NKJV)

When we allow fear to stop us, it is a clear sign that we do not understand the love of God. When you know how much God loves and cares for you, you are not afraid. He is with you, fighting for you, defending you, protecting you, and working on your behalf. As His love becomes perfected in you, fear will leave. If you struggle with fear, meditate on Scriptures that talk about the love of God. The more revelation you have on the fact that God loves you and is with you always, the harder it becomes for fear to operate in your life.

Third, a sound mind is a weapon to use against fear. Where does fear attack? In the mind. In fact, science says that the brain has a fear center but God is saying that you have been given a sound mind. This means that you have control over your mind.

God has given you the ability to control the thoughts that you think. Whenever a fearful thought comes to mind, immediately cast it down and replace it with God's Word. To cast down a thought you simply say, "I cast down every thought that is not of God in Jesus Name." You can say it out loud under your breath, or if you do not have privacy, you can say it in your mind. Then choose to think on something from God's Word such as one of the Scriptures quoted in this chapter. If, for example, you receive a fearful thought about becoming an entrepreneur, once you cast that thought down, you can then speak something such as, "God is with me and I will have great success. Nothing can stop me or cause me to fail because God is on my side." Keep thinking these positive, Bible-based thoughts intentionally throughout the day.

Since fear has stopped countless dreams, make it a priority to annihilate fear from your life. This is spiritual warfare. To get to where God wants you to be, you need zero tolerance for the devil in your life.

To end your struggle with fear:

1. Cast it out of your life through prayer.

2. Ask God to deliver you.

3. Learn as much as you can about the love of God. Tell yourself all day long that Jesus loves you. Meditate on how great His love is for you and how He is on your side. He will protect you and bless you.

4. Take control of your thoughts. Do not allow fear to put thoughts in your mind. Instead, cast them down right away and replace these negative thoughts with the Word of God.

5. See yourself doing the things you are afraid of. See yourself back in school, running your own company, living in your mansion, etc. Envision your success and you performing extremely well.

Fear comes to stop you and to hold you in bondage. Fear keeps its victims locked in a cage so they have no freedom and cannot move as they should. We know that when Jesus came, he set us free from all bondage. Therefore, fear has no right to keep us trapped. In fact, the enemy's operation in our lives is spiritually illegal. It is the same as someone breaking into your house and stealing from you. They do not have a right to do this, but they took advantage of an opportunity, such as a weak lock on a door.

For the devil to gain entrance into your life and steal from you, he relies on fear. When you become afraid, it means that you are not trusting God. So your faith, whether in part or the whole, has shifted to something else. This is dangerous because whatever you believe, you will receive. So if fear can get you to believe you will fail, then you actually might fail, not because you did a bad job but simply because you expected to fail. What you set your mind on will be your reality. Be careful what you fear, because you certainly do not want that to become your reality.

I would like for you to think about this. Why is fear working so hard to stop you? Why is fear in overdrive to keep you from doing the things that are in your heart to do?

I will tell you why. Your future is already determined in the spirit realm and fear is aware of it. Fear knows that if you step out and start that business, you will actually be very successful. Fear knows that if you launch this ministry, you will reach many souls and bring destruction to the kingdom of darkness. Fear knows that if you go back to school, speak out, start that non-profit, and just step out and do that scary, "I-have-no-idea-how-this-will-work" thing, that you will actually be successful. You will grow and bloom into a whole new you. This is what fear wants to stop – the transformation you will experience from stepping out and being brave.

And this is why you cannot let fear stop you any longer. You have to fight back. You must denounce the lies fear has told you all these years and choose to trust in God. Even when it is scary and you cannot see your way – trust in God. He is with you and will help you. In several places in the Scripture, God tells us not to be afraid for one reason – that He is with us. That is all the reason you and I need. Our Heavenly Father is in us and with us so what can overcome us? Nothing.

Below are Scriptures you can meditate on daily to overcome fear. Remember, to meditate on God's Word means to mutter it out of your mouth. You do not need to be loud. A whisper will do. When in public and cannot speak out, you can speak to yourself in your mind. It is still very powerful and effective.

The LORD is my light and my salvation— whom shall I fear? The LORD is the stronghold [strength] of my life— of whom shall I be afraid? Psalm 27:1 (NIV)

The LORD is with me; I will not be afraid. What can mere mortals do to me? Psalm 118:6 (NIV)

Be strong and of good courage, do not fear nor be afraid of them; for the Lord your God, He is the One who goes with you. He will not leave you nor forsake you. Deuteronomy 31:6 (NIV)

Say to those who are fearful-hearted, "Be strong, do not fear! Behold, your God will come with vengeance, With the recompense of God; He will come and save you." Isaiah 35:4 (NIV)

But now, thus says the Lord, who created you, O Jacob, And He who formed you, O Israel: "Fear not, for I have redeemed you; I have called you by your Name; You are Mine. Isaiah 43:1 (NKJV)

Yea, though I walk through the valley of the shadow of death, I will fear no evil; For You are with me; Your rod and Your staff, they comfort me. Psalm 23:4 (NKJV)

I sought the Lord, and He heard me, and delivered me from all my fears. Psalm 34:4 (NKJV)

When I am afraid, I put my trust in you. In God, whose Word I praise – in God I trust and am not afraid. What can mere mortals do to me? Psalm 56:3-4 (NIV)

So do not fear, for I am with you; do not be dismayed, for I am your God. I will strengthen you and help you; I will uphold you with my righteous right hand. Isaiah 41:10 (NIV)

For I, the Lord your God, will hold your right hand, saying to you, "Fear not, I will help you." Isaiah 41:13 (NKJV)

Do not be afraid; you will not be put to shame. Do not fear disgrace; you will not be humiliated. You will forget the shame of your youth and remember no more the reproach of your widowhood. Isaiah 54:4 (NIV)

There is no fear in love. But perfect love drives out fear, because fear has to do with punishment. The one who fears is not made perfect in love. I John 4:18 (NKJV)

Please head over to the Workbook to complete your personal exercises for this chapter and continue the destruction of fear in your life.

CHAPTER 9

The Faith and Mouth Connection

"Death and life are in the power of the tongue, and those who love it will eat its fruit."
Proverbs 18:21 (NKJV)

Several years ago, I had a dream. In this dream, I saw a garden filled with young green plants. The plants were very well organized in rows and were thick and full. Then suddenly, I saw my hand reaching to pull them up from the ground. I woke up and began to seek the face of God through prayer. I needed to understand the dream. The Lord showed me the interpretation and I want to share that revelation with you.

The plants in the dream were things that prayer and faith over the years were creating for me. They might not have been manifested in the natural, but God created them in the spirit realm, and they were growing and flourishing. My hand pulling the plants out of the soil meant that my faith was dwindling and as such, was destroying my blessing.

I needed to learn more from God, specifically, what actions have I performed that were uprooting that which I had built over the years through faith. God showed me that as a result of my faith decreasing, my thoughts and words changed. The words I recently started speaking were working against my prayers and were undoing what God was getting ready to do for me. I thought this was a powerful revelation and I worshipped the Lord for being so Loving and Wonderful that He would reveal this to me so that I would learn from it and stop making this mistake.

Many times we do and say things, but do not understand the effects they have within the spirit realm. As human beings, we are powerful spirit beings, and our spiritual lives take precedence over our natural lives. The problem is we see, feel, and know the natural more than the spirit and as such, the temptation is to prioritize the natural realm over the spirit realm.

> *"Death and life are in the power of the tongue,*
> *and those who love it will eat its fruit."*
> Proverbs 18:21 (NKJV)

Your words go before you and prepare a future for you. Do you want to change your future? Then change your confessions. Change your words. Speak the life you want into existence. But this happens by faith. When you believe that God has more for you, you speak it out of your mouth and your consistency and faith will cause the seed of that word to grow and manifest in your life.

You must remain true to your confessions. You cannot confess health prosperity, marital prosperity, financial prosperity, and other good things, and then speak against them. Your negative words will uproot your seed. Your heart and mouth must be in agreement with the plan of God for your life. Otherwise, your words have the potential to destroy what God is intending to perform in and through you. This is what God was saying to me through the dream. He was warning me to watch my words so that I do not destroy my upcoming blessings.

I am sharing the same message with you. Be mindful of your private confessions and your public conversations. Do not speak against your marriage and spouse when you are trusting in God to give you a prosperous marriage. Do not speak words that condemn you to poverty when you are praying to God for financial prosperity. Do not confess, "my head is killing me" when you are believing in God for good health and long life.

The Bible makes it clear,

> *"Out of the abundance of the heart, the mouth speaks."*
> *Matthew 12:34 (NKJV)*

Your words are a product of your heart and what is in your heart comes from the seeds that were planted there. Whether the Word of God, or seeds of thorns such as the wrong music, TV programming, cultural and family values, social norms, and the like. Nothing can come out of you that is not first planted inside of you. This is why it is important that you are extremely careful with what you allow to enter you. Take caution with what your eyes see, your ears hear, and anything that enters you. But God has given us a way to fight bad seeds - His Word. If you fill your heart with the Word of God, the power of the Word is released when you speak and it goes to work on your behalf.

As we read in Proverbs 18:21, life and death are choices and represent the only options for the type of life you can live. It makes it richly clear that your words have the power to create two destinations for you - life or death. The future you live in is determined by the words you speak today. There are three takeaways I want to highlight in this verse:

1. Your tongue (words) contain power. Remember this the next time you open your mouth to speak.

2. The tongue produces two things - life or death. There is no grey area. Every word that comes out of your mouth either creates life or creates death for you and those around you.

3. There is no avoiding the consequences of your words, whether they were spoken intentionally or unintentionally. You will eat the fruit of your words if you continue to speak them. You cannot get away from that principle. There is a law of Seedtime and Harvest in the spirit realm, which means we reap what we sow (Genesis 8:22). Our words are seeds. You cannot pray against the words you have sown, especially if you are continuing to speak those negative words. It just does not work that way. You must repent and change your confession. If you have sown in death, you need to change your confession to life.

Many Christians speak death over their ideas before they even get started. They doom themselves to fail right at the beginning because of the words they speak.

When the Israelites were freed from bondage and were wandering in the wilderness, God appeared to them with these two options. As we discussed before, the older generation that did not have faith in God had died and their children were now being prepared by Joshua to move into the promised land. God spoke to them with this warning,

> *"I set before you life and death, blessing and cursing, therefore choose life that both you and your descendants may live."*
> *Deuteronomy 30:19 b, c (NKJV)*

Here, we further see that the option of life and death can also be interpreted as obedience or disobedience to God. Life comes when we walk in obedience to God and death comes when we disobey. The clearest example of this is salvation. When we believe in God and obey His Word unto salvation, we have eternal life. When we disobey and do not believe in Jesus Christ as our Savior, we have chosen eternal death (John 3:16).

In Deuteronomy, we see that this also applies to the lifestyle available to the Israelites. They could obey God and possess their dream life or they could disobey because of fear and the lack of faith, and as a result, have death. Now, this does not mean they would have fallen and died right away. What it means is although they would have breath in their lungs, their lifestyle was that of death because they were not living the life God had designed for them.

You could have spiritual life through your faith in Christ and still be dead because you are not living out the destiny God prepared for you. You are alive but at the same time dead. It seems that many people die decades before they are actually buried. To live life outside of your purpose is to not live at all.

You must come alive to your destiny. You must come alive to your dreams. Your destiny came from God and He intends for you to fulfill it. It is one of the ways you are fruitful in the Kingdom of God and is your contribution to society. It covers everything from your spiritual life, your marriage and family life, your ministry and service to others, your finances and wealth, your career and businesses, and everything else that concerns you. God wants you to prosper in every area of your life.

If the Israelites chose to disobey God and not possess the promised land, they would have been physically alive but really dead, because they would not have lived the life God planned for them. Their spirit is stagnant and unsatisfied, making no progress forward. They would have walked through Earth and not fulfilled their destiny, walking on a path that does not lead to prosperity throughout all areas of their lives; a path that was not carved out for them. This is death. It does not mean you go to hell. Your salvation has saved you from hell. I am speaking concerning the lifestyle you live while you are on Earth.

Notice that God told the Israelites, if they chose life, both they and their children will live. Your decisions impact the next generation. You probably wish your parents were multi-millionaires who owned several multi-million-dollar companies that they could have just passed down to you. Wouldn't life have been so much easier! The choices of the parents affect the children. So today, make good choices that leave blessings behind for your children, whether they are already born, in the womb, or will be born in the future.

Your children should not face the struggles you faced. You are the curse breaker in your family and your children will be reapers of blessings because of the decisions you have made. Let the next generation only know of your struggles through the stories you tell them, yet may they never experience these hardships.

Your time here is very precious and extremely limited. Most people do not live to see eighty years old but in eternity we will live forever - we could be wishing you a happy 10,000 birthday. Compared to that, life on Earth is very short. You must spend your time wisely. Do not continue to waste time on things that do not lead to your dream.

Decide to break out of the dead life and create a plan to enter your dream life. It may not be easy, but it will be easy. It may not be easy because we are creatures of habit. We love our routines even if they are against our destiny. On the other hand, it will be easy because God is with you and He will help you. It is easier to flow into your dream life because you are doing what you were designed to do. Doing what you were called to do is always easier than fitting into someone else's mold.

So, with life and death set before you, what do you choose?

Please head over to the Workbook to complete your personal exercises for chapter 9. You will need a partner for this activity and remember to have fun with it!

CHAPTER 10

Go Forward

"And the Lord said to Moses, 'Why do you cry to Me. Tell the children of Israel to go forward.'"
Exodus 14:15 (NKJV)

O K. So now it is game time. You have the tools to change the old mindset towards money, you have broken generational curses of poverty, you have learned some savvy money handling tips, and you have even crushed fear, built up your faith and aligned your words to match, and discovered the greatest secret to creating wealth. Now what?

Now is the time that you go forward. It is unto you according to your faith, as Jesus taught those who sought miracles from Him. You see, you can learn many wonderful things. You can attend all the conferences and seminars in the world. You can even read every book there is on a subject; but if you do not have faith, then it provides little to no benefit.

"For indeed the gospel was preached to us as well as to them; but the word which they heard did not profit them, not being mixed with faith in those who heard it. For we who have believed do enter that rest..." Hebrews 4:2-3 (NKJV)

The Scripture above is in reference to the rest of God, which we discussed in chapter seven. We see here that those who believed entered the rest (the promised land) but those who did not add faith to what they were taught received no profit from it. For the Word of God to benefit you, you must have faith in what you learn. If there is no faith, then the Word brings no profit to your life.

My beloved brother and sister in the Lord, please go forward. Walk in faith and believe the Word of God concerning you. Fear, doubt, low self-image, and everything negative have stopped you long enough. It is time to enter your realm of unstoppable.

1. Make notes of the things you want to change in your life based on what you have read in this book. If you have the workbook, you have already been doing this.

2. Decide on your avenue to wealth based on what God has spoken to you. If you do not feel like God has given you specific instructions (such as "start a business in XYZ"), then make note of your ideas and dreams. Which are you most passionate about? Which one is on your mind most often? You have something within you that God can use to build wealth. Write all questions that you have and things that you need to learn about the area you have decided to pursue. Then purpose in your heart to learn as much as you can about it. Seek wisdom and obtain it.

3. Keep your faith up, trusting in God always.

4. Do not let the old mindsets of bondage hold you down but cast them down and think God's way.

5. Prepare yourself to obey Him. Meditate on His Word and tell yourself that if you hear His voice obey right away.

6. Always obey God. Do not think about what He said, do not try to figure it out, and do not attempt to make sense of it. Most times, it will not make sense to the natural mind. Just obey Him and do so right away - no ifs, ands, or buts about it!

7. Do not speak against your prosperity. Let your confessions align with what you desire from God.

8. Go forward and do everything your heart desires with prayer and following the Holy Spirit. Start your business, go back to school, start investing, build your budget, work on your 401K and retirement income, start investing in real estate… and so on.

Now is the time to start doing. I hope that within one year or less, I hear testimonies from all of you on what great things God has done in your lives. I can imagine you a year from now enjoying your life and living in much more abundance than you are right now. I can see your increase. Like Caleb finally received his mountain when the Israelites entered the promised land forty years later, I see your mountain and your promised land; and by now, you do too.

Here is an example to help you:

Because I like things to be very clear, I want to create this story to help you.

Ariella has always wanted to design clothes and create a clothing line. She comes from a very poor family and has no resources to do this. She has never known anyone who was successful at anything. But this dream of designing clothes is just not leaving her. She does not believe she has heard the voice of God, but after reading this book and going through the Workbook, she realizes that this dream was planted in her by God. Although she did not hear a loud voice like in the movies, she now sees God has been speaking to her heart all along. She decides that every day she is going to pray for God to help her make this dream a reality.

One day as she is praying, she feels like she should sketch out her first line of clothing. After prayer, she goes to a Dollar Store around the corner and gets a sketchpad and pencils. She prays for the Holy Spirit to give her ideas. As ideas come to her mind, she writes what she is feeling and thinking and then begins to sketch her designs.

After a week, she is done. She says, "God, what's next?" She realizes that she needs to get someone to make her designs for her. She works overtime to get some extra cash and pays someone to create three of her designs, which, after trying very hard, are featured in a local fashion show. God, working behind the scenes sends an investor to the show. Before the investor's arrival, God had already planted ideas of Ariella's designs in his mind. When the investor sees her outfits on the runway, right away he says, "this is what I have been looking for," not knowing that God is the One who gave him the liking for Ariella's designs. God also closed his eyes to the other designers' works so his focus is only on Ariella's. Ariella strikes a deal with an investor who will give her funding to create her first season of clothing.

Ariella now sells her clothing online, has employees working for her, and has a six-figure salary. She then gets another dream of seeing her clothing in department stores. With hard work and the help of God, that dream happens more quickly than she was expecting and she is now making millions of dollars a year. She is now branching out into designing shoes and jewelry. Her dream keeps on growing, that is, her seed produced fruit with more seeds in itself, which keeps producing more and more fruit.

Here is another example:

Mike never had dreams for himself. He came from an environment where he just had to work. He has a job, a good one and he makes $20,000 a year. He is learning a lot and likes it. He reads this book and uses the accompanying Workbook and begins to pray to God to show him His plan for his future. He wants to prosper but does not know how.

Mike has lots of ideas for his company, although he is not the owner. These ideas get stronger and his confidence increases. Mike hears from God, "go to school and get a business degree". He is not sure if it is God or not, but he feels peace every time he prays about going to school. He also feels afraid because he thinks he is not smart enough to go to college. He pushes past fear and enrolls in night school. He motivates himself to study and finish his program, not taking any semesters off. He graduates and lands a management job at his company.

Then God says, "go back to school and get an MBA." He does it. Fast forward to the future, God sets things up so that Mike is now the Chief Operating Officer managing over 500 employees and makes $425,000 a year, not including his lofty bonus and other benefits. Everyone loves working on Mike's team. He is kind, caring, honest, and displays the Word of God in the way he works and treats others.

He owns two homes and three cars, has access to the company's private jet, and financially supports twelve missionaries who are delivering the Gospel of Jesus Christ in foreign countries. Because God wants us to prosper in all areas of our lives, Mike is married with three children. He even has a local organization that teaches young boys how to grow up serving God and overcome the temptations of this world.

God gives Mike wisdom and he has this idea to invest in real estate. Though he feels nervous to do this, he walks by faith and steps out on this idea. He begins purchasing property and renting them for a profit. He is inexperienced in real estate and made some mistakes with his first property. He does not let that stop him. Instead, he learns from every mistake and continues to acquire more and more properties until he owns several properties across many towns. Through this, Mike earns an additional $30,000 a month and owns 12 properties, which are worth $10,000,000 combined. He and his family could live off his real estate income, but he loves working for his company and bringing God's Kingdom to that organization.

Mike is the only one in his family to go to college or have any kind of success. But now that he has broken that family curse, his children are better positioned to prosper. It is much easier for them because their dad has already paved the way by the power of the Ultimate Father, Daddy God.

I hope at least one of the stories that I created inspires you in some way. What will your story be? Take some time and give thought to the question. When you have arrived, I will be celebrating with you.

Please head over to the workbook to complete the work for this chapter. Have fun!

A Letter to Myself

Dear [Insert your beautiful name here],

I am a wonderful creature made by God to dominate and rule. I was never created to be poor, average, powerless, or to settle. Inside of me is destiny, which was planted by God before I was even born. God knows my dreams and heart's desires and He desperately wants to give them to me. He wants to make my dreams come true.

This is the time where I now stop doubting God. I have no more fear or doubts. God is with me so I cannot fail. Yahweh holds my hands and I cannot be defeated. There is greatness inside of me so I go forward and do great things. Today begins a new day for me. I see the sun breaking through the sky. This is the moment I move out of the land of bondage and take hold of everything God has for me. Nothing can stop me. Nothing can block me. Today, I become unstoppable in Jesus' Name. All my dreams will come true. My story has changed, beginning today, with this moment.

And when I have arrived at my dream life, I promise to never forget Jesus Christ my God, to serve Him always, to remain humble before Him, and to love all His people.

Best Wishes for the Best Future.
Standing with you as you prosper, your sister,
Jeanel D. Champion

Bibliography

[1] Strong, James. *Strong's Exhaustive Concordance of the Bible.* Abingdon Press, 1890.

[2] "Nephesh." *Bible Study Tools.* Old Testament Hebrew Lexicon – King James Version. Web. 2020.

[3] "Charis." *Bible Study Tools.* New Testament Greek Lexicon – King James Version. Web. 2020.

[4] "Restore." *Merriam-Webster.com.* Merriam-Webster. Web. 2020.

[5] Monopoly: the property trading board game. Hasbro / Parker Brothers. (1986).

[6] Mint. Intuit, 2021. Web. 2 October 2021.
Mint is a registered trademark of Intuit.

[7] Dave Ramsey. *Ramsey Solutions.* 2020.
Dave Ramsey is a household name in personal finance, debt elimination, and wealth building.

[8] The Motley Fool. Stock Advisor. www.fool.com. 2020.

[9] Robinhood Markets. https://www.robinhood.com. 2020.

[10] Acorns. https://www.acorns.com. 2020.

[11] Stash. https://www.stash.com. 2020.

www.ingramcontent.com/pod-product-compliance
Lightning Source LLC
Chambersburg PA
CBHW031954080426
42735CB00007B/386